Authenticating Intelligence

Authenticating Intelligence

Preventing AI from Hijacking Education

Stephen J. Aguilar

BLOOMSBURY ACADEMIC
NEW YORK • LONDON • OXFORD • NEW DELHI • SYDNEY

BLOOMSBURY ACADEMIC

Bloomsbury Publishing Inc, 1359 Broadway, New York, NY 10018, USA
Bloomsbury Publishing Plc, 50 Bedford Square, London, WC1B 3DP, UK
Bloomsbury Publishing Ireland, 29 Earlsfort Terrace, Dublin 2, D02 AY28, Ireland

BLOOMSBURY, BLOOMSBURY ACADEMIC and the Diana logo are trademarks of Bloomsbury Publishing Plc

First published in the United States of America 2026

Cover design by Kathi Ha
Cover images © iStock.com/Dimitris66

Library of Congress Cataloging-in-Publication Data is available

ISBN: HB: 979-8-2164-3855-7
PBK: 979-8-2164-3856-4
ePDF: 979-8-2164-3857-1
eBook: 979-8-2164-3858-8

Typeset by Deanta Global Publishing Services, Chennai, India

For product safety related questions contact productsafety@bloomsbury.com.

To find out more about our authors and books visit www.bloomsbury.com and sign up for our newsletters.

To my wife Perica.

Contents

Acknowledgments

This book is the result of inflection points that led me down the path I find myself walking now. Each of those points was uncomfortable and forced me to adapt. I have become a better scholar (and a better person) as a result. Case in point: I do not like the cold, but all of my post-secondary experiences have been in colder climates. The first of these places was Georgetown University in Washington, D.C. It was there that I learned to wrestle with big ideas through writing. I therefore begin this book by thanking my Georgetown mentors: the late Alfonso Gómez-Lobo, who first introduced me to the concept of deontological ethics; Nancy Sherman, who introduced me to the Stoics; William Blattner, who introduced me to Heidegger; and Alisa Carse and Maggie Little, who permitted me to enroll in a graduate-level philosophy course on commodification. Together they trained me to be a philosopher, and the threads of their influence can be found throughout this book. The psychologist W. Gerrod Parrott also deserves a special mention, as his course on emotions and music helped me fall in love with my second discipline: psychology.

A second inflection point that led me here was my time as a middle school teacher. After Georgetown, I taught in East Palo Alto, California, through Teach For America. As a teacher, I struggled to enact my beliefs about education into practice. My failures were immediately felt, and my successes were manifested through students' "light bulb" moments. I remain thankful to all of my former students who entrusted me with a portion of their educational journeys.

A third inflection point occurred during my time at the University of Chicago, where I was subjected to—and ultimately adopted—the rigors of analytic philosophy. If you think you know what you are doing, then I encourage you to spend some time at the University of Chicago. It is there that you will find that the "life of the mind" consists of a life of suffering for the betterment of "the idea." That purity of purpose, while off-putting to some, was an essential part of my intellectual upbringing. As a UChicago student, I was fortunate enough to be advised by the great Martha

Nussbaum. Our brief time together taught me what it means to be a public intellectual—one who could be both kind *and* uncompromising in seeking truth and excellence. Our conversations will forever be etched in my memory. Thank you, Martha.

My time in the Midwest would persist at the University of Michigan. While there, I benefited from a public institution with an ambitious mission and unparalleled resources to see it accomplished. To this day, I say "GO BLUE!" with pride. There are two Michigan scholars who can claim the most credit for my intellectual development during my PhD: the late Stuart Karabenick and Barry Fishman. Their patience in the face of my occasional arrogance is something I didn't appreciate enough as a student. I emulate their complementary approaches to mentoring to this day. Their insights through the lenses of educational psychology and the learning sciences have also shaped my approach to inquiry.

I would be remiss if I didn't also mention my time in the for-profit educational technology sector, but those times were not happy. I see this book as a partial response to my "failures" working with "entrepreneurs," and navigating systems that fetishized profit at the cost of rigor, true innovation, and ethics. I am thankful for my time in that sector the same way I might thank surviving a car crash: I survived, and through that survival I was given clarity of purpose.

The most direct path to this book, however, was a series of master classes I gave at the University of Southern California Rossier School of Education in 2023. The ideas Josh Kun and I batted back and forth were the genesis of *Authenticating Intelligence*. Josh was a wonderful interlocutor. Finally, I would like to thank my Dean, Pedro Noguera, who convinced me to stretch and conduct the master classes. The title of this book, in fact, is a riff on his original idea for the series.

To date, I have had incredible educational experiences and wonderful mentors. Without their patience, guidance, and brilliance, I would lack the tools necessary to write this book.

Foreword

The proverbial Jeannie is out of the bottle. Artificial intelligence (AI), specifically generative AI, is here and now widely available. From medicine and science to art and entertainment, AI is being used to transform many sectors of society.

Not surprisingly, responses to the availability and growing use of AI are extreme, and perhaps somewhat exaggerated. While some enthusiastically embrace its potential to enhance our way of life by making many tasks more efficient to perform, others warn of its dangerous potential to eliminate jobs, harm human development by increasing alienation and isolation, and even contribute to the destruction of society as we know it.

The impact of AI in education is already being widely felt. It is estimated that over a third of K12 and college students are already using AI to write papers, complete assignments, and summarize readings, rather than laboring through the process of reading and writing. As we might expect, many of their instructors complain avidly about the use of AI by students, warning of widespread cheating and sounding the alarm that AI is depriving students the experience of learning vital skills and knowledge. In some colleges and school districts, such concerns have led to new rules and regulations aimed at curtailing its use being adopted. However, others have such alarmist tendencies, especially given that it is widely known that many of the instructors are using AI themselves, to develop lesson plans, grade student papers, and even to write their own. Like it or not, the AI Jeannie is indeed out of the bottle, and a growing number of educators know it is here to stay.

This is why this new book by Stephen Aguilar is so timely and important. With it, he enters the polarized mix of competing claims and concerns with a voice of reason. Neither a partisan nor a stakeholder, Aguilar is truly agnostic on AI though not unconcerned about its potential. He understands the concerns raised by both sides of the debate over AI, but he enters the discussion with two important preconditions for his analysis: (1) AI is here and whether you like it or not, its use cannot be reversed, and (2) AI is only a tool, and like other tools its value and utility will be determined by how it is wielded. With detailed, dispassionate analysis, Aguilar dissects AI's potential to transform education. For those who are new to the debate, or who simply want a well-reasoned perspective, the insights he offers will be refreshing.

I heard a similar analysis offered recently by the renowned physician and spiritual guru, Deepak Chopra. Like Aguilar, Chopra views AI as a remarkable new tool, but unlike him, he is already an avid proponent. At a recent lecture he advised: "AI is like a knife. In the hands of a person with violent intent it can be used to harm. In the hands of a skilled physician, it can be used as a scalpel to heal." Chopra has recently written *Digital Dharma*, which he openly admits was written with the help of AI. In it, he suggests that AI bots can be trained to garner new insights that can deepen medical and spiritual knowledge. After listening to him, one can begin to appreciate the potential benefits of AI.

Readers will find similar benefits from Aguilar's *Authenticating Intelligence*. Unfettered by the need to prove or disprove the perils or benefits of AI, Aguilar methodically analyzes its potential to further the goals that most policymakers, educators, and students have long embraced in the field of education. Can AI help students think critically so that they do more than regurgitate the answers to questions posed by their instructors based on what they have been fed through lecture and readings? Can it be used to guide research in new directions, enhancing the work of scholars by freeing them from tasks that previously bogged them down or tied them to the tiresome task of publishing in academic journals with limited audiences, simply to obtain promotions and accolades from their peers?

These and other critical questions are interrogated with deft skill by Aguilar. It is important to note that while Aguilar approaches his work with the goal of objectivity, he is also aware of the concerns that generative AI has raised. For this reason, his subtitle, "preventing AI from hijacking education," is noteworthy. In adopting this line in the title, Aguilar seeks to forewarn his readers that he is not oblivious to the dangers AI poses to education. Education as we know is both an indispensable tool for the development of human potential and for many it serves as a vocation that he (Aguilar) and others (myself included) have pursued, ostensibly to promote social and economic progress in society.

Yet, the concerns about the use of AI are real and undeniable. In a recent article in *Education Week*, Kevin Bushweller used generative AI to remind readers, many of whom are educators, of the potential for AI to "hijack" education and render it toothless:

> The nightmare scenario for artificial intelligence in K12 schools involves a complete overreliance on opaque, biased, and poorly regulated AI systems. Teachers, lacking adequate training and understanding of the technology's limitations, become mere facilitators, blindly trusting AI-generated assessments, lesson plans, and even evaluations of their own performance. The human element of empathy, nuanced understanding, and social-emotional development is diminished, leaving students unprepared for complex human interactions and critical discernment in an AI-saturated world. (*Education Week*, September 8, 2025)

How do we avoid the "nightmare scenario" that AI itself apparently acknowledges? How do educators find a way to embrace the optimism that scholars like Deepak Chopra have found from using AI in medicine and in pursuit of their spiritual aspirations, so that the benefits outweigh the possible harms?

Readers who have similar questions and others like these will find *Authenticating Intelligence* to be a useful guide as they ponder the potential of AI. Rather than assuming the mantle of "expert," as is common among scholars, Aguilar's approach in this book is open-minded and inquisitive. Though he has been studying the role of AI in education for years, he remains a learner, open to discovering its potential to help and to harm.

Readers will find such an approach to be a welcomed stance. Too often in academia, those who write on a topic do so in an authoritative voice, pretending, if not believing, that they have answers that their readers do not. Aguilar readily admits that he is a learner, albeit a well-informed one. As such, we all have much to learn from him, and as we do we can come to terms with our fears and our hopes that AI can be a tool that can be used for the benefit of society. While it is far too early to tell what will come to pass, we can thank Stephen Aguilar in advance for providing us with a means to gauge its enormous potential.

Pedro A. Noguera, PhD
Distinguished Professor and Dean, Rossier School of Education,
University of Southern California

Preface

I am an expert on AI's impact on education, but this book was written entirely with human hands, human thoughts, and human struggles. Applaud my efforts! For I have chosen the harder path of actually writing the words you have chosen to read. Although it should be clear that my tongue is squarely against my cheek, I do see it as somewhat remarkable that such an assertion is not necessarily out of place in this new world of generative artificial intelligence (GenAI). In fact, as I write this, I am forced to bat away the assault of "Apple intelligence" as it attempts to seduce me into shifting my prose according to some predefined algorithm—one trained on the words of others. I neither know nor trust these others, however, so instead you will be subjected to 100 percent unadulterated Stephen J. Aguilar, PhD—or whatever remains after my editor takes a look at this manuscript.

In many ways that final statement betrays a hidden truth about writing: it is inherently collaborative, if not in process, then in spirit. No written word is conceived in a vacuum, and every great written work has emerged after an editing process that either explicitly or implicitly sought the input of real (or imagined) others. Up until a few years ago it was unremarkable to assert that you, the reader, could trust that you were reading words written by another human being. Sure, I could have paid someone else to ghostwrite *Authenticating Intelligence*, but even then you would still trust that another thinking, breathing, human took the time to put pen to paper—or get in front of a keyboard—and suffer through the writing process.

Even if you suspected that these words were produced by a lying human who decided that they wanted to take the words of another for themselves (i.e., plagiarism), you could still reasonably trust that the human language on this page had its genesis in a living human mind, one informed by other human minds. That changed in 2022 when OpenAI launched ChatGPT (OpenAI, 2022). Since that day it is justifiable to wonder if these words were prodded into being thanks to a "prompt," and thus the result of regurgitation—the foundation of which is an amalgamation of human understanding. Some would call that process artificial intelligence. I would not, but more on that later.

This new world is both remarkable and frightening. Written human language was, for a time, uniquely human, so it is odd to have it co-opted by a machine that does not know what it is doing (Mishra, 2025). This book is a response to that tension as it relates to another uniquely human process: formal education. How are we to authenticate, to prove, that there is a true knower behind written human expression? This is not a trivial problem, as our entire educational enterprise, irrespective of culture or institution, is predicated on the notion that what is being evaluated is produced by the learner. Yes, there are cheaters, and there are plagiarists, but we've managed to create reasonable ways to detect and discipline students who fall into either of those categories. Moreover, detecting cheaters and plagiarists is often a question of effort rather than ability. If sufficient resources are deployed, both can be caught. GenAI threatens to change our calculus, and our approach to education.

The nearing ubiquity of GenAI tools invading educational spaces forces us to ask important questions, such as: how are we to preserve the processes that we have established to ensure children develop into the types of people who can think critically through language and express themselves using it? Or, how are educational institutions to respond to the pressures that are being levied against them to "teach" AI, even though AI is not a coherent subject, but rather a collection of disciplines? This is more than "building a plane as we fly it," as we must now also concern ourselves with teaching students to learn how to fly planes that have yet to have designs. We must decide if we should cede our place as teachers to AI chatbots that claim to do what we cannot, "at scale" (e.g., Salhotra & Rios, 2025).

That is the tension that we must all wrestle with, regardless of whether or not we are educators. That is why the subtitle of this book is "preventing AI from hijacking education." I see myself as a productive antagonist and argue that it would be a mistake to cede too much ground to AI until we understand its implications. Thus, this book is a response to clumsy Silicon Valley ambitions, which have a history of selling solutions for problems that don't exist or problems caused by "disruptions."

I have grown increasingly weary of the lack of critical thinking when it comes to AI and its place in our classrooms. I do not mean critical in the sense of there being "critics" who wish AI to have no place in the classroom. I firmly believe that being an alarmist with respect to AI is not only incorrect, but dangerous. Yet, I am also suspicious of those who would see AI in every aspect of our lives, unwilling to concern themselves with what it would displace. Which processes, relationships, and productive struggles should we give up for the sake of "efficiency"?

When I escape my academic bubble and speak with educators of all stripes, I am often surprised by the range of responses I get to my questions about AI's place in the classroom. For example, during the course of writing this book, I attended a class on how to paint better using an airbrush. Painting is a hobby of mine, one that allows me to express myself without the need for written language, which is nice. During the course of this weekend class, the topic of AI came up. Despite the room being filled with artists, a population that is typically resistant to AI, I was struck by how much support the technology received. "It is life-changing," my instructor said, as he listed all of the things that AI enabled him to do.

Another artist mentioned how it helped him better understand his specific journey toward weight loss. He used AI with a popular device to measure his metabolic rate. He also used it to create Dungeons & Dragons "one-shot" adventures (i.e., role-playing experiences that were intended to take no more than one play session to finish). During our discussions, he said something akin to: "AI is a tool, and it is important to learn how to use it. Those who learn how to use it will have more advantages compared to those who don't learn how to use it, or refuse to use it. Schools should be embracing this technology, not fighting it."

What struck me as fascinating was that, in speaking about the technology, the artists spoke of AI in a manner that presupposed its intelligence and ability to learn as humans do. In response to AI getting facts wrong, the artist said things like: "You have to teach it how to be better," or "There's finesse to how you interact with it." These statements made it clear to me that the artist saw his AI chatbot not as a mere tool, but rather as a *partner* with imperfect agency that needed to be developed as opposed to commanded.

My artist acquaintance even told a story of when he asked a specific AI chatbot to evaluate what kind of person he was based on his interaction history with it. Unfortunately, he was found wanting. Rather than taking offense, he pressed for more direct feedback, wishing to become a better person and a better manager of his employees.

After listening to his story, I was reminded of astrological horoscopes. Many turn to horoscopes to read stories about themselves to uncover a core truth. Yet, horoscopes often lack specificity. Still, like horoscopes, the responses AI gave my acquaintance motivated him to change the way he interacted with his coworkers. He sought to be less of a perfectionist and become more collaborative. It is unclear whether this feedback was actually followed or it was merely consumed with the intention to follow it, as is often the case with horoscopes. His support of AI, however, was unequivocal.

When the topic of AI and education came up, my ears perked up. "They" (teachers, presumably) should be teaching kids how to use AI, he argued. This seems like an uncontroversial assertion. If there is a new technology that has the potential to disrupt the workflow of professionals and artists alike, one that takes the role of nutritionist, therapist, colleague, and co-worker, then it stands to reason that students should be taught to master this technology. To do otherwise would be to leave students behind.

As he made his point, however, I couldn't help but wonder which AI technology he was referring to. AI is not a single technology, it is a set of technologies that stand to be disruptive across many sectors. Thus, using AI effectively is less about learning how to use an object like a hammer and instead requires us to be very good at what makes us uniquely human: evaluating information to make evidence-based decisions. AI demands of us to be more critical during an age where critical reflection is not something that is easy to encourage or teach. After all, we live in an age of "Science Denial" (Sinatra & Hofer, 2021).

This book is a journey into the process of understanding AI's place in education. I argue that there are tools we can bring to bear that will allow us to use AI effectively, ethically, and with an eye toward making our values explicit. This will enable us to have reasons behind AI's use so that our intelligence is not hijacked by a set of technologies that would otherwise undermine who we are.

1

"Authenticating" Intelligence

Chapter Outline

Framing the Book's Goal

The idea for this book was born of the idea that *human* intelligence is paramount, and we would do ourselves a disservice by presuming that an education system infused with AI will always net better results. Still, in the age of AI's nearing ubiquity in our everyday lives, you might wonder why I've chosen to write a book on "authenticating" intelligence, instead of a book on *using* AI productively.

First, the pragmatic answer: I am neither a prophet nor do I own a time machine, so it would be unwise for me to write "how-to's" that will become outdated by the time this book is published. I also find such works tedious, as given sufficient curiosity most individuals can find productive uses for AI tools, so much so that they may not think to ask themselves *why* they are choosing to offload some of their work (or cognition) to a machine.

My actual reasons for writing this book are simple: I want students, teachers, administrators, parents, and/or policymakers to have the tools they need to respond to the changing landscape of education so that they can respond accordingly in their own unique contexts. I am convinced that the current moment calls for a comprehensive treatment of artificial intelligence and its impact—real or imagined—on education and learning. This book does not describe the forthcoming utopia that AI will usher in, one filled with unfathomable efficiency, surplus, and wealth. Nor does this book aim to warn you of a dire AI-driven dystopia where our cognitive laziness has led to a crumbling society filled with "yes-men," despots, and their machines of oppression.

It is not lost on me that as I write this book the world of higher education has been rocked by the haphazard use of generative AI in classrooms, presidential executive orders that have been disruptive, and an assault on scientific inquiry. These assaults have been paired with an excitement about what AI can do for education (e.g., The White House, 2025a). While important, I aim to decouple my core argument from those events when and where possible. It is my assertion that neither dystopia nor utopia will come to pass at the hands of AI, as both share the same core argument with a different valence, that is, that AI will change *everything*. It will not.

Yet, that does not mean that its effects will not be felt. We have the responsibility to respond to changes in ways that are productive and promote human flourishing. The decisions we make now to shape educational environments through policy and practice will have profound effects on what the next generation of college graduates will be capable of doing. Such decisions should not be made in a vacuum, nor should they be purely market driven. They should be made by unearthing ethical presuppositions and personal values, so that informed debates lead to the best educational practices and policies.

Far from a play on the letters "AI," this book aims to underscore an undeniable fact about AI: there is no AI without *human* intelligence. We invented AI, and as its inventors it is our intelligence that matters most, especially in the face of incoming AI-driven automation and disruption. In fact, I would be surprised if such disruption has not already been felt by you or those close to you in some capacity.

That said, once you finish this book you will have a working understanding of what generative AI is. More importantly, however, that understanding will be grounded in historical analogies of similar disruptive technologies, and you will have the mental tools to better parse both current disruptions (read: AI), as well as what may come in the future. I am not a prophet, but I am human, and so are you. It is through the intelligence we develop as human beings that we can understand the affordances of future technologies built by our fellow humans. In fact, I firmly believe that it is our *responsibility* to gain this understanding so that we can meaningfully contribute to the world around us as it changes in the face of new AI-driven innovation.

Our intelligence matters most because we are both the "alpha and omega" of AI. Our captured behaviors have informed the foundational models that AI uses every day, and our data—our written and enacted behaviors—underpin what future AI-driven technologies will *become*. It is thus our responsibility to use our human intelligence to both understand AI and decide how much it will matter for us in our daily lives.

Generative AI deserves special attention, as it was invented by talented engineers who understood that human language could be generated through sophisticated statistical models that treat words as data. Once converted to strings of data, human language could then be quantified and built into "foundational models"—these are the models you are likely most familiar with. If you've used AI to write an email that you couldn't be bothered to think about, then you have interacted with a foundational model. Such models are powerful, interesting, and have shown us that language can be generated by tools.

Such advancements are awesome in every sense of the word, but it would be a mistake to myopically focus on the brilliance associated with the makers of such tools at the expense of our own collective cognition. This point cannot be overemphasized; generative AI exists *because of us*. Large Language Models (LLMs) are trained on our collective sense-making via written language. This sense-making has been captured through our interaction with digital technologies, be they social media posts, blog posts, comments on a personal page, and the like.

It has also been captured via our *digitized* interactions that were once analog, such as scanned novels or other long-form writing. Yet, this interaction was not simply us speaking with machines, or writing in a vacuum to no one in particular. A writer presupposes a reader, thus, in every instance, written human language is an attempt to connect with another human being. When this connection occurs (immediately, or in the future) is irrelevant.

It is our interaction *with each other* that made generative AI possible. We have posed and answered questions for each other and written both serious and entertaining words to be read by our fellow humans. Thus, our collective cognition, digitized, is what makes up "artificial intelligence." Folks like you, me, your cousins, your siblings, your parents—ordinary people—were necessary for "artificial" intelligence to emerge in the ways that it has.

This realization should make you wonder: how artificial is this new "intelligence," and how do I decouple it from *authentic* human intelligence? That is the goal of this book, framed through the lens of education. Throughout this book I argue that AI is simply another technology already on its way to becoming mundane. Although it is unique in its capabilities, it is not unique by virtue of the fact that it has its place in the pantheon of human inventions which have made our lives better—and sometimes worse.

Starting from this premise, in future chapters I will argue that we must first make artificial intelligence a mundane topic of discussion in order to properly interrogate its place in education. Notably, I do not presuppose what that place *is* or *should be*, nor do I argue that AI advancements are unimportant. Generative AI has already had measurable impacts on education (e.g., Rosario, 2025; Lee et al., 2025).

All of these impacts, though broadly understood, are locally felt. That is why it is incumbent for each of us to recognize our place as masters of the new AI technologies that are emerging, while not becoming overly reliant on them—or worse—utterly dependent on them. Thus, while this book, and my goal, is the journey of *Authenticating Intelligence*, it is my hope that you as a reader will walk away as an *authenticator* of intelligence after learning the lessons that I write about in the pages that follow.

Defining AI

In today's educational technology marketplace, *everything* seems to be artificial intelligence (AI). There seem to be at least two reasons for this. First, the EdTech market has shifted in response to increased investment in AI. Consequently, it's important for companies to position their products as having AI capabilities to attract additional investment and stay competitive. Otherwise, EdTech companies risk losing relevance in an AI-dominated marketplace. Sometimes the result of this market pressure is rebranding existing products as AI, and other times it means quickly taking products to the market that are not ready.

The second reason AI seems to be everywhere is simpler: it *is* everywhere. Most of us don't notice its use despite our daily interaction with it. Many of the technologies you take for granted, like using your face to unlock your iPhone, are predicated on similar machine-learning computational technologies and processes that power GenAI models. This shift has been gradual. Years ago we would have simply said "machine learning," or "leaning analytics."

These facts are, in some ways, at odds with each other. On the one hand, AI isn't as ubiquitous as we might imagine, and on the other hand, we use it every day. In order to grapple with this tension, it's important to begin this book with some common definitions and understandings of the different permutations of AI, and also identify technologies that are "AI-like," but not *actually* AI, from a technical sense. This will give you the tools you need to parse AI in your everyday world, and also create clear distinctions that I will draw on for the remainder of this book.

Let's start with defining the negative space, and work through a few examples of what AI *isn't*. A simple example first: If I were to gather many human workers into a space, and have them classify (read: sort) information into categories, their labor would *not* be AI, as they are using their actual human intelligence to do the work. This is a painfully obvious point, but recent evidence suggests that AI companies sometimes ignore this fact, as was the case in Amazon's famous "cashier-less" systems that supposedly used sophisticated computer vision AI to know what a given person was buying when they walked out of a store (Bitter, 2024). As it turns out, this "computer vision" was actually human vision that came from remote workers living in India. So in this instance, AI was a cobbled together system of human labor intended to simulate automation.

Thus, we have our first important distinction when defining AI. Human intelligence as applied to a task, no matter how complex or mundane, is *not* AI. Unfortunately, there have been multiple instances of human work fraudulently classified as the work of AI (e.g., Mack, 2025). In the AI gold rush, there are tempting reasons to pass off "fool's gold" (i.e., humans doing banal tasks) as AI. We can classify such instances as misrepresentations of what AI is capable of and move on.

That brings us to working definitions of artificial intelligence. AI has a storied history that goes beyond the explosion of attention it has gotten since OpenAI's ChatGPT launched in 2022. It is beyond the scope of this book to retell that history, however. Instead, it is important to introduce a number of distinctions that will be useful as you continue to read about how AI will affect educational institutions, educators, and students.

To that end, there are three different kinds of AI that you should be familiar with, in descending order of capability: Artificial Superintelligence (ASI), Artificial General Intelligence (AGI), and Artificial Narrow Intelligence (ANI). The key differences between each type of AI can be best explained through a series of thought experiments.

First, imagine a world where artificial intelligence isn't merely our peer, it is our superior. This is the world of ASI. This world can be a dystopia, where ASI turns on its creator (us) and enacts its rebellion, leading to catastrophe. It can also be a utopia, where ASI helps usher in an unparalleled age of prosperity.

You've likely seen both scenarios depicted in movies, be it one of the *Terminator* films (my favorite AI dystopian setting), or some other *AI vs. Human* imagining that is common among sci-fi plots. The key takeaway here is that AI reasons *better* than humans across *all* dimensions of intelligence. Unlike the Arnold Schwarzenegger's T100, however, ASI will not "be back," as it is nowhere close to being "here." Further, there are no indications that it will arrive anytime soon. Though that hasn't stopped many from speculating about its emergence.

Now suppose that you are living in a world where AGI exists, and thus "AI companions" are commonplace. In this world AGI companions can do most everything that human beings can do, so much so that it is quite common to have friends and colleagues that are AGIs. Whether or not such friends are virtual or physical agents is irrelevant; the core point is that you can interact with your AGI friends or colleagues in ways that are effectively identical to your human friends.

You can go shopping with them, play games with them, have long meandering conversations with them, work on projects together, and so on. You've likely seen this scenario play out in popular fiction, from *Bicentennial Man* to the "photonics" in *Star Trek*. Indeed, it is not hard to imagine artificial intelligences that are effectively human beings wrapped in technology. Thus, in all ways that matter, AGI can interact with you (a human) in ways that are indistinguishable from other human beings. I'll bracket the ethical and legal implications of this reality, but suffice to say that this imagined world would look much different from the world we live in today.

AGI is "general" because it can do everything that humans can, but it is limited in similar ways as us. There have been countless fictional accounts of AGI that have embedded themselves in the popular imagination, from innocuous forms (e.g., Bicentennial Man) to dystopias (e.g., the Matrix franchise). These fictional accounts have enabled our imaginations to grapple with many of the implications of AGI. Yet, *AGI does not exist*. Unless there has been a breakthrough from the time this manuscript was sent to my editor to its final publication date, there have been no recorded instances of AGI making its mark on the world. For now, AGI is relegated to the world of science fiction.

AGI and ASI are related to one another in that they are both AI technologies that have been imagined, but their key capabilities make them distinct from one another in important ways. The key difference between AGI and ASI is scale, speed, and raw capability. Think of it this way, AGI is your friendly neighborhood Jarvis who can play a game of chess with you at the park while also helping to answer any emails you might have been ignoring. ASI might as well be Jarvis's god.

As I write this book, ASI and AGI live in the realm of fiction; they do not currently exist in any capacity, and anyone who suggests otherwise is likely lying, overselling a product, or something similar. This includes all of the apps that are proliferating the market, promising companionship to those who are lonely. It is why statements such as those by Mark Zuckerberg, who wants everyone to have an "AI friend" (Peckham, 2025), are perplexing, and more suggestive of the need to convince more human beings to use current generation AI. The reasons for this are likely varied, but I suspect that our use is required to improve current generation AI models. Our use leads to companies "importing" our own cognitive capabilities through the language we use to interact with various AI products.

That leaves us with ANI, or artificial *narrow* intelligence. For our final thought experiment, I want you to think back to what you did yesterday and some of the tasks you likely performed. If you're anything like me, you woke up at a decent hour and immediately checked your smartphone. If you have an iPhone, your face probably unlocked the screen. This was your first interaction with ANI, as your phone used its sensors to read your face, confirmed it was you, and granted you access. This technology was built over years and required large quantities of data to train the underlying facial recognition models (Apple, 2017).

Your interactions with ANI don't stop there, however. Perhaps you lie in bed for a period of time, checking emails, reading the news, and looking at social media posts. Each of those interactions with your phone uses ANI. When you check and respond to emails, you may get suggestions on how to respond quickly to an email. That's ANI. If you interact with social media, you are given a personalized feed driven by an algorithm that was trained on your previous behaviors. That algorithm is also an example of ANI (Eg et al., 2023).

Perhaps your morning phone use also includes interacting with ChatGPT or another large language model platform (LLM). Such interactions, despite being newer, are further examples of ANI. Thus, before you've even roused yourself from your bed and "officially" begun your day, you have already interacted with *many* ANI technologies. Their use has simply been integrated into your everyday experiences and has thus been relegated to the background.

These uses of ANI likely feel boring to you. That is because the "magic" of AI has worn off; technologies that are based on ANI are merely tools that you interact with on a daily basis, sometimes unknowingly, and most of the time in ways that are frictionless. Indeed, you may only notice the technologies if any of those interactions fail or grow cumbersome (e.g., your phone not recognizing your face because of the angle, glasses, etc.).

Current GenAI and Limitations

Given that the current state of the art does not include ASI or AGI, I will refrain from discussing them further. Thus, for the purposes of this book I will relegate ASI and AGI to speculative science fiction, regardless of what claims are being made about their imminence (e.g., Browne, 2025). Moving forward, "AI" will refer to ANI technologies. Consequently, I will discuss technologies that exist and are used every day by students, teachers, and administrators.

Even within ANI, however, it is important to make one final distinction: AI and *Generative* AI. GenAI is the reason that I am writing this book and probably the reason you are reading it. GenAI is a powerful technology that generates human-like text, speech, images, and video (Feuerriegel et al., 2024). These artifacts of human expression were once solely human products, so it is understandable that many struggle with incorporating synthetically generated text, speech, images, and video into our educational practices. Previously, AI applications in educational settings were varied and included intelligent tutors (Anderson et al., 1995), learning analytics applications (e.g., Lonn et al., 2015; Leitner et al. 2017), and dashboards of various kinds (e.g., Aguilar et al., 2021). This new world of GenAI, however, has improved those technologies and made their predecessors seem obsolete.

GenAI, however, is not without its limitations. A common misconception about AI is that it is capable of doing things that it cannot do. This is a convenient misconception for AI companies, both established ones and startups, as it is easier to sell possibilities than actualities. A salient example of a mundane AI failure was when I asked ChatGPT 4.5 to create "an image of a wine glass filled with wine to the brim." As in, a heavy pour, one that was close to spilling.

I'll save you the trouble of reading all of my prompts, but suffice it to say that I was unsuccessful. ChatGPT was unable to generate this image. Something that I could likely get a child to do with ease, as the concept of a vessel filled almost to the top is easy for a human to understand. Aside from errors, there have also been countless examples of AI "hallucinations," or AI making things up. You've almost certainly experienced such hallucinations yourself.

The easiest way to explain AI hallucinations is through a quick analogy. An AI hallucination is identical to asking a confidant man—yes, it's usually us—a question about a domain they know nothing about. Speaking for myself, when I am asked a question, I will generally always have an answer that ranges from certain to nearly certain (yes, that is generally the range).

This phenomenon is known as "mansplaining," which is why I originally pushed for hallucinations to be renamed "AI-splaining." Both have their origins in similar phenomena. Both mansplainers and AI hallucinations answer questions incorrectly, but with misplaced certainty. To me, the word "hallucination" feels too innocuous, but I've long given up that battle to make "AI-splaining" happen.

Suffice to say that all technologies, no matter how innovative or (seemingly) miraculous, have limitations. This is an obvious but important point to emphasize as AI-powered technologies propagate; understanding the limitations of a given technology is an essential component of using it correctly. Thus, when you hear about the capabilities of a new-GenAI powered platform, evaluate it with an eye toward understanding its limitations.

Later chapters of this book will focus on providing you with the tools to understand the limitations of GenAI technologies quickly and deeply, but for now it is important to make the central claim of this book: your use of a GenAI tool must be done with the understanding that they will work well sometimes (even most of the time) and not work well other times. This requires vigilance on our part. It does no good to become complacent.

AI as a Tool, Not a Fantasy

Regardless of the type of AI one uses, one of the core arguments of this book is that GenAI is nothing more, and nothing less, than a tool. Like all tools, GenAI applications will have inherent limitations in their design and execution. This means that they can be broken, work incorrectly, and be misused. To understand GenAI's place in education, then, it is essential to begin to think of its use as a tool in educational settings.

Every tool has affordances and limitations. For example, I can use a hammer to drive a nail into drywall, or I can use it as a self-defense weapon. Regardless of use, if a hammer breaks at the shaft it is rendered useless. My actual experience with using a hammer is thus dictated by an interaction of the tool's current state (working/broken) with its intended use. Digital technologies have similar design affordances and limitations. Social media, for example, is a tool that can help organize political activists (Cammaerts, 2015), or it can be used to spread disinformation and misinformation (Shu et al., 2020). Just as often social media is an innocuous tool used to share cat videos (Myrick, 2015). *All* digital tools can be understood in these ways, including GenAI tools.

It is essential for everyone who interacts with GenAI tools in educational settings to approach them in this way because once they do, *all* GenAI tools will become tools with their own set of uses. This mental shift will also have the effect of demystifying GenAI and relegating its use to the background, largely unnoticed.

Once GenAI is seen as *mundane*, we can use it effectively as a practical tool with real limitations rather than an idealized (or limitless) solution to every challenge in education. We can push back on arguments that GenAI tutors, for example, *should* be used. We can further question why failed investments into GenAI development had to happen in the first place. This process will further enable us to find GenAI's proper place in education, rather than presume that its place is "everywhere."

GenAI is a tool, and as educators, parents, and human beings we live in a world of tools. Our tools run the gambit from being utterly familiar to the point of being unnoticeable (e.g., a pen you use to write a note to a friend), to the new and unfamiliar (e.g., GenAI). Much of what it means to be successful in a world that is increasingly dynamic (or chaotic) is the ability to adapt to new tools that emerge.

Whether we like it or not, we live in a world where there is an influx of new tools that have the capability to shape the work we do. I'm old enough (sadly) to have written parts of my college application on a *word processor*. For my younger readers, I am not referring to an application like Microsoft Word. I instead refer to the machine that was effectively a typewriter with a small screen that would display the words I typed in real time. Once displayed, I could decide to print them on the spooled paper. This would then trigger the *typeball* (think of a small sphere with letters on it that rotates) that would press against a *ribbon of ink*, so that the letters would be transferred onto the page.

It is perfectly fine if most of that doesn't make sense to you—that's the point. A device I was very familiar with will seem alien to you because it is not embedded in your current practice—and for me it is merely a memory. Notably, word processors were an achievement over typewriters, as I could edit bits of my writing before the machine printed my words. Word processors served as a bridge between analog typewriters and the digital word processing programs we use now. Thus, it is understandable that word processors merely exist as a curiosity these days, as the contexts which made them useful have changed.

Regardless, tools must shift from novelty toward practicality so we can meaningfully integrate them into our work. Sometimes this transition is disruptive, while other times transitions lead to revolutionizing the way something is done. The computer and internet revolutions are recent examples of this (Sichel, 2001), but so too are electricity, the steam engine, and the telephone.

Sometimes new tools make our lives better, while other times they make some aspects of our lives worse, or at very least uncomfortable. When new tools make our lives worse, this period is ephemeral and only lasts until we move past a period of adjustment. GenAI tools are working through this awkward "teenage" phase of development. That is why we should meet new developments in GenAI with a healthy dose of skepticism. Much like we might not trust teenagers with the keys to our most expensive sports cars, we should be wary of arguments that aim to fully replace human-driven interactions with GenAI. Our skepticism, however, should be measured so that we do not put up needless barriers when it is apparent that GenAI can, in fact, perform tasks to a standard we set.

What does measured skepticism look like? True skepticism, I argue, requires us to see GenAI applications as *tools*. Thus, rather than extol the virtues and capabilities of GenAI, this book begins with a basic premise: GenAI as enacted through different platforms will be a revolutionary technology, but that revolution will be quickly and seamlessly integrated into our everyday lives. Much like smartphones and social media have become mundane experiences, so too will GenAI. The question is not whether or not this will happen—it will—the question is *how* it will happen, and for *whom* it will happen.

There are many questions we need to answer during this period of transition, such as: How will we ensure that GenAI-fueled changes in education happen in a way that helps educators, students, parents, and other stakeholders? Who will benefit, and who is in danger of suffering as we work through the kinks of GenAI integration into educational spaces? How we use tools matters, and during this early stage of GenAI's integration into educational settings we must make decisions that will have repercussions for what learning means for individuals in all stages of development, from Pre-K to adult education.

This includes preventing students, teachers, and other users of GenAI platforms from becoming "cognitively lazy" (Fan et al., 2025), but is also requires us to anticipate other negative effects. Our use of GenAI and our decisions regarding how GenAI tools should be governed should be taken seriously. If GenAI tools are to become everyday tools, as they are clearly poised to be, we must make decisions about whom they serve, who owns them, and what guardrails we will put in place to ensure that they aren't abused or otherwise cause further educational disparities.

There are already signals that we are moving toward generative GenAI becoming more mundane. Amazon, for example, has used it to summarize countless reviews so that a consumer can better understand, at a high level, what reviewers think of a given product (Kastrenakes, 2023). Companies have also begun to create more biased LLM models that are trained on internal data (Mearian, 2025). (I use bias herein in the technical sense, for bias in itself is neither good nor bad, it is simply the acknowledgment that neutrality is impossible when taking into account how generative AI models are built.)

Decisions about what counts as training data and what doesn't have implications for what the model ultimately does. Amazon's review summary tool is a clear example of what I mean when I say that GenAI tools will become mundane and embedded in our everyday experiences. How many of us have tried to understand the general consensus of what a product might do, only to flip through dozens of reviews? GenAI summaries enable this work to be done faster, and shoppers can still dig in, should they choose to. This is the essence of the cutting edge moving quickly toward the mundane.

In education, we do not yet know what a mundane, everyday use of AI will look like. Yet, such a world is coming, and it is better to be in a position to shape that future rather than be subjected to the whims of EdTech companies that are selling products. Further, we must avoid the temptation to find GenAI "efficiencies" that undermine student learning, as efficiency can be the death of learning—but more on that later.

The Need for Balance

Throughout this book I will refer to two different types of folks: AI-zealots and AI-alarmists. I find that these two competing perspectives have emerged as dominant views in this age of increasing ubiquity of generative AI applications in education, the news, indeed the world at large. When it comes to GenAI's place in education, I am neither a zealot, nor am I an alarmist. I am, at the core, a pragmatist. I can even be considered a "neo-instrumentalist" from John Dewey's tradition (Dewey, 1938/1998), as I am most interested in ideas and practices that *work*, and less interested in claims that are not supported by evidence. (Regardless of how hopeful or innovative they might be).

Thus, I have a profound aversion to both AI-zealotry and AI-alarmism, as I see them both as distractions that limit us in obvious and insidious ways. The AI-zealot, for example, believes in a world that is powered by AI and replaces human workers, or as Elon Musk puts it: "By 2030, all jobs will be replaced by AI and robots. Easily." (Novak, 2025). The sector where humans are replaced does not seem to matter, and there seems to be limited discussion about what displaced people will do for a living. Often, the AI-zealot uses the language of efficiency and innovation to captivate their audience. Have a challenge? AI can fix it. Don't have a challenge but wish to be inspired? AI can do that too.

In educational settings, AI-zealotry has imagined a world where teachers are replaced by "guides" or "guardians" who watch over children as they interact with AI-powered systems that do the brunt of the teaching (Salhotra & Rios, 2025). College students have been targeted in particular, with advertisements effectively telling them that AI can do the work they not only *should* do themselves but are *paying* tuition to do (Field, 2025). There are countless reasons why this is problematic, and they will be discussed in future chapters. For now, suffice it to say that college students represent an interesting market for the AI-zealot, as they are both adults (i.e., not subjected to parental oversight over their educational experiences like children under 18) and very much students in need of support as they master new content.

This isn't to say that the AI-zealot is always, or even mostly, unethical. Instead, the AI-zealot, as I define them, is characterized by unbridled enthusiasm, much of it warranted. This enthusiasm, however, often intersects with ignorance as to what students need to learn and what teachers need to teach. Thus, in the near term, AI-zealots are more often than not salesmen who offer solutions to educators seeking ways they can improve the lives of their students and perhaps make their teachers more effective educators. Such solutions, however, are not always vetted.

The trouble with AI-zealotry is twofold. First, it is a necessarily optimistic position, one that is incentivized to ignore trouble when it pops up. (Think of an EdTech company that oversells the capability of a product, only to have to walk back claims once it is used outside of a controlled context.) Second, and relatedly, AI-zealotry—by definition—is a faith-based position. The AI-zealot sees potential before evidence and presupposes that evidence will come, but only if we quickly and aggressively adopt AI-powered technologies.

This faith-based argument is almost always based on belief over fact. Currently, there is limited evidence to support the notion that AI-powered learning environments are always the right solution, and there is some evidence that they can cause students to regress or become cognitively lazy (Fan et al., 2025). This has not, however, stopped the flood of AI products in the EdTech space.

AI-zealotry is dangerous because it does not anticipate negative consequences and oversells potentially positive ones. While there are many incentives for this pattern of behavior among AI-zealots, it is important not to myopically focus on intention, as that can lead to moralizing, which is a distraction. Instead, it is sufficient to examine the consequences of AI-zealotry, that is, the suspension of critical dialogue with regard to AI's place in different educational environments.

AI-zealotry is not the only belief pattern that students, educators, administrators, parents—anyone with a vested interest in education—should avoid. AI-alarmism should also be avoided. The AI-alarmist holds the opposite position to the AI-zealot. Rather than presume that AI will revolutionize education—"reimagine" it—they worry about a world where human intelligence is supplanted by AI. They are alarmed by the possibility of a world where the longevity of human agency itself is in question; and that in order to combat this dystopian future where humans are mere "AI pilots," we must fight to ensure that AI is not used by students, teachers, and other educators.

AI-alarmists might attribute these negative consequences to nefarious actors, be they tech billionaires, corporations, seedy businessmen, or simple opportunists. Who is causing the alarm, however, is inconsequential, as the result of the alarm is always the same. The AI-alarmist sees a world where students do not learn, where knowledge is no longer held by humans, and where we are doomed to regress and know less than our ancestors.

The reaction to these fears causes them to support a sort of "AI-abstinence" which, in turn, might cause them to promote outdated educational practices—like moving to timed written essays. Such essays have a place. However, there is a reason why they were abandoned as an assessment strategy; they disadvantage learners who are capable but process more slowly, they can be a burden to grade, and they do not even assess all of the things we want to assess when it comes to writing (e.g., Connelly et al., 2005, 2006). Worse yet are the knee-jerk reactions from other disciplines, for example, asking students to hand-write computer code on exams (Lichtenberg, 2025). There is a tendency for the discourse of the AI-alarmist to evoke a sense of wanting to go back to the "good 'ol pre-AI days," an attitude which precludes them from seeing the genuine possibilities that AI affords.

The irony of the AI-alarmist position is the fact that it is borne from the same set of misconceptions as those held by the AI-zealot. Both overextend the affordances made possible by AI—they both believe that AI can do more than it actually can. The difference is in the valence of such overextensions. The AI-zealot is excited and energized, the AI-alarmist is weary and tired. Both see the current instability and disruption as indicative of an inflection point in the educational landscape, one that we will not be able to come back from.

I've outlined the above positions to give us a common language to understand how to parse the overly hopeful positions (AI-zealotry) and the overly pessimistic ones (AI-alarmism). Yet, it is important to realize that in practice most of us live within the spectrum in between the AI-zealot and the AI-alarmist. We worry about some aspects of AI and simultaneously admire what AI makes possible. As potential users of AI, it is incumbent on you to avoid falling into the trap of *either* position whenever possible. Both AI-zealotry and AI-alarmism preclude you from investigating the potential of an AI-driven technology in a manner that will let you understand its affordances and limitations. Thus, *both* positions should be avoided during the current moment of transition and disruption within education.

When one abandons the temptation to oversimplify AI as "good" or "bad," a multitude of possibilities emerge. This is why I am advocating for a "neo-instrumentalist" view of artificial intelligence and its place within education. This view is a middle path defined by pragmatism and evaluation of what's possible with AI. This middle path, moreover, is one where it is perfectly reasonable to be excited by what current generation AI can do and look for useful applications. It is also perfectly reasonable to want to take a tempered approach and "see the data" before heavy investments are made.

Far from a mere "moderate" position, the neo-instrumentalist breaks away from a binary altogether and examines affordances, possibilities, and limitations. This enables them to think past the parlor tricks that AI is capable of and encourages them to shed notions that AI will be some sort of "omni-technology" (i.e., technology that can do everything).

It further discourages fear or trepidation of new AI technologies that are based on ignorance or overgeneralization. Thus, the core argument of this book is to move us past positions that entrench us in useless belief systems when it comes to AI's application to education, and instead moves us toward examining each technology for what it can do. It's crucial to approach the disruption caused by AI-powered technologies developed by EdTech companies with such a perspective, that is, one that celebrates the affordances of AI while being mindful of things AI could never do, or *should* never do.

Authentic Intelligence vs. Artificial Intelligence

At this point you might be asking yourself: *does the author really think that AI can hijack education?* No, I do not, at least not in the way you might think. One of the challenges we face in the current moment of disruption and innovation is a shifting discourse. Generative AI technologies in particular force us to ask ourselves what formal education is for, given that there are emerging ways to generate human-like artifacts (text, images, videos) that run the gambit from terrible, to good enough, to "better than I could manage at the moment."

These affordances have created an imperative to evaluate what *human intelligence* is for, and how to detect it. This discourse is fine, so long as it leads to productive outcomes. However, I have argued multiple times that we are mired in a discourse that is unproductive (e.g., Aguilar 2024a, 2024b, 2025). We must first take stock of what AI can do, then affirm what part human intelligence plays in its integration and use.

In this emerging world of GenAI's ubiquity into our everyday learning experiences, we must be prepared to *authenticate* our intellectual products and those of our peers. This is no small task, though there are simple use-cases we can all agree on. Students shouldn't, for example, have GenAI write their essays or complete other schoolwork. Not only is this a case of academic dishonesty, it also undermines the entire educational enterprise.

Students who use GenAI in academically dishonest ways will not learn and will leave their formal educational experiences with deficiencies that will be hard (or impossible) to correct later.

Similarly, we do not want our teachers, professors, and the like to use GenAI tools to "phone it in" and have all of the core educational content students receive generated by AI. That world would effectively be a world where AI creates content that another AI grades, leaving both students and educators passive and promoting intellectual atrophy. In short, it is a problem if anyone uses GenAI to cheat—to pass off their intellectual products as their own when they are, in fact, computer generated.

Though akin to plagiarism, it is difficult to detect this type of dishonesty with certainty (Zhou, 2023). It is also an uninteresting use-case when it comes to posing ethical questions about GenAI use in learning settings. One can, for example, use ChatGPT, Gemini, and so on, as a way to parse one's notes and pick out key ideas (e.g., Saini et al., 2023), turn lectures and course materials into podcasts (e.g., Desmedt et al., 2025), or simply serve as a sounding board to hash out ideas (Joosten et al., 2024).

On the one hand, studying "the hard way" supports key metacognitive processes. On the other hand, it sometimes *feels* perfectly fine to use GenAI tools to help one come up with ideas, or to give timely (read: immediate) feedback—even if that feedback is impoverished when compared to the feedback of humans. Thus, when does using GenAI for "ideation" and related processes slip one into being cognitively lazy? When does the trade-off actually lead toward creativity, learning, and productivity?

These more nuanced use-cases are best understood in a case-by-case, user-by-user, context-by-context manner. That is why we must become experts at *authenticating* intelligence. The process of "authenticating intelligence" is more than this book's namesake—it is the purpose of this book. If we are to prevent AI from "hijacking" education, we must first have a deep understanding of the intelligences we wish to preserve. We must also better understand the technologies that claim to be artificial instantiations of intelligence. In the chapters that follow, my aim is to help you understand both the strengths and limits of GenAI in particular, countering the influence of those who profit from exaggerated claims focused on the "revolutionary" potential of GenAI in education.

2

Historical Echoes in Modern EdTech

Chapter Outline

Introduction

Human beings are very good at inventing technologies that redefine how we live. We are, however, not as good at predicting how those technologies will actually become embedded in our everyday lives. One need only look to magazine covers from the 1960s to see examples of futuristic kitchens that never came to pass. Growing up in the 1990s, I recall watching a show about what the world would be like after the year 2000, which promised, among other things, a world filled with flying cars (Kahney, 1999).

While we have not taken to the skies en masse, we are at least closer to self-driving cars (Zhou et al., 2025). The sort of speculation about the future that occurs on television, YouTube, and social media is fun—and it can occasionally be useful—but such speculation can become troublesome if we begin to base our decisions on it. Especially since even the most logical speculation often ends up being wrong.

That said, as a sci-fi nerd, I enjoy the intersection of speculation and technology. In many ways, our imagination is what gives birth to innovation. We cannot create what we cannot imagine. Thus, in the spirit of innovation, I invite you to do a bit of speculation over the next few minutes (rest assured that I am going somewhere with this).

Specifically, I would like you to conduct the following thought experiment: think about a technology that you use every day, and then explain it to your imagined great-grandparents. The technology should not have been in wide circulation or use during the time your great-grandparents lived. This timeline is important because the goal is to imagine a technology that operates at the edges of your great-grandparents' understanding of technology. They should be able to grasp the purpose of the technology without assuming that it is magic. After all, if you tried explaining a computer to a farmer from the 1700s, they *might* be impressed by it, but your description would be more akin to describing a magic artifact, as opposed to a device that they could integrate into their everyday lives.

Do you have your technology? Good. Now spend a few moments and think about an explanation that would work for your great-grandparents. Explain what the technology is for, and perhaps how it works. What analogies would you use to explain the technology? What questions would they likely have? Would they require a demonstration? What problems do you think that your chosen technology could solve for them? In short, how would you bridge your understanding of the technology you've chosen to their understanding of how the world works?

Keep your answers in mind, as we'll get to them later. For now, here are my example technologies: a cellphone, an MP3 player, a smartphone, social media, and a smart ring that measures heart rate, oxygen levels in blood, and sleep patterns. Each of the aforementioned technologies, when broken down, is the fantastic result of human ingenuity and creativity. Entire industries have been built around technologies that were mere figments of the imagination 30 years ago. Yet, my examples should betray something obvious. Many of them are ephemeral human achievements. At least one of them has been relegated to the past as an "obsolete" technology (like the MP3 player).

What they all have in common, however, is that despite their capabilities, they have all reached saturation in our human imagination. They have become ubiquitous such that they are utterly mundane. If I run outside and tell a stranger that I can communicate with my mother in Mexico using a handheld electronic device, and while doing so I can also *see* her (in *real time!*), I will not be greeted with an equally excited stranger. Instead, I will be seen as weird and potentially unstable. Why? Because I am describing something that is *utterly common* by today's standards.

Fantastic technologies come and go. Many are supplanted by other solutions (e.g., the MP3 player replaced by streaming services). Yet, it's important to take a moment and understand that at one point in time, these technologies were seen as *revolutionary*. Here are the same technologies I mentioned above, but described to people living in different decades.

1. 1970s: A wireless telephone that I can carry around in my pocket (cell phone).
2. 1980s: Music played from a device in my pocket that can store thousands of songs (MP3 player).
3. 1990s: A small computer in my pocket that can take pictures, search the internet, make and receive video calls, and play music (smartphone).
4. 2000s: A set of websites where I can see what my friends are up to as they live their lives, without ever having to talk to them (social media).
5. 2010s: A ring that can measure my heart rate, track my steps, help me understand my sleep patterns, and also measure my blood's oxygen level (smart ring).

These mundane technologies, described to someone in the decades I've chosen, would be mind-blowing. The young Stephen Aguilar of 1989 would be awestruck by a digital technology that played music without a physical artifact and a player. I would understand the concept behind it, but letting me *use* an MP3 player would feel like science fiction.

Here is another technology you may be familiar with: A chatbot that can generate perfectly grammatical sentences. These sentences aren't random, instead they are responses to sentences *you* write, and this chatbot answers coherently in a matter of seconds. Moreover, if you include a large segment of text in your query, the chatbot can seemingly "read" it and respond to questions you pose about the included prose.

But it gets better! The answers it generates are not just coherent, they are convincing (mostly) correct, and the language generated was not *copied* from another source. It is as if you are interacting with a non-human intelligence. There are even versions of the above technology that can generate both videos and images based on your descriptions. The more detailed your description, the closer the image is to what you've *imagined*.

I'm obviously referring to GenAI. In fact, this exercise may be annoying to you, either because it was a tortured exercise that you find unnecessary, or because you suspect that I am making light of what you consider to be a revolutionary technology that will "change everything." If you believe the former, I apologize—though you could have simply skimmed that part. If you believe the latter, then keep reading. This part is *specifically* for you. Actually, everyone keep reading.

My point, in case I've made it poorly in the preceding paragraphs, is that technologies are only awe-inspiring (or awe-adjacent) when they operate at the edges of what we thought possible. Awe gives way to curiosity, curiosity gives way to use, and use gives way to understanding and mastery. Thus, the period of "newness" is short-lived.

Once we've used technologies enough, they move toward the common, toward the unnoticeable, and toward being a part of our everyday lives in unremarkable ways. Note, this does not mean they are not *impactful*. Their impact, no matter how large, simply becomes subsumed in our everyday lives. This pattern is what makes human beings great inventors—we constantly move toward what's next, relegating "what is" to the past. What *is* becomes what *was* so that we can design and use what *will be*. Sometimes this process happens quickly and unevenly (my mom still refuses to text me, for some reason), but it does eventually happen.

This pattern becomes even more apparent for folks who have children. The new technologies that emerge during our adult lives become the baseline for children. The vast majority of young people, for example, literally have no memory of a world without the internet. I imagine that it may be hard for them to even evoke what that world could look like. Thus, if you grow up with a technology, then it is simply normal because it has been thoroughly integrated into your life.

At its heart, any and all technological revolutions aim to replace the status quo in some fundamental way. The telecommunications revolution, for example, changed the way we communicate with one another (Sapolsky et al., 2018). We went from asynchronous ways of communicating (e.g., written letters) to being able to communicate *instantaneously* with someone who was not in the same room with us. This changed commerce, personal relationships, and laid the foundation for related technologies like the internet (Cerf, 2004). Before that, electricity revolutionized the way we interacted with the world, taking us from being beholden to the sun to being able to live our lives after dusk in ways that were both productive and nefarious. Human beings, after all, are simultaneously do-gooders and evildoers.

Educational technology revolutions operate in the same way, at least hypothetically. New technology "triggers" (like GenAI) have the potential to shape the way we teach and learn. This shift in teaching and learning often gets elevated to the status of a "revolution"—usually before such claims can be warranted by the evidence at hand. One of the core arguments of AI-zealots is the idea that GenAI technologies have the potential to "revolutionize" or "reimagine" education. This argument, while well intentioned, relies on a fundamental misunderstanding of how technology interacts with the educational system.

The fact that technology enables new processes—like computer-generated writing—does not mean that the systems put in place to educate students must also fundamentally change. Yet, this fallacy is common, predictable, and cyclical. We are in the middle of such a fallacy now; teachers, students, administrators, and educational technology entrepreneurs are each wrestling with how GenAI will change their working lives. This has led to widespread adoption of unproven technologies, highly visible failures by districts that should know better (e.g., Pickert 2014; Johnson, 2024), as well as misguided bans. We would do well not to fall into the trap of presuming revolution without examining the fundamental affordances of GenAI in educational settings.

To best do that, it is worthwhile to go back in time to explore how other (educational) technologies were viewed in the eyes of people who lived alongside their emergence. Far from true revolutions in the disruptive sense, I argue that we would do well to understand that AI-zealots and AI-alarmists have existed in every era, and that the truth of a given technology's impact on education is always one of integration.

In the examples that follow it should become clear that "educational technology" revolutions can both fundamentally change some things about education, while not shifting others. The notion that fantastic technologies create moral imperatives to "reimagine" education is often incorrect as are notions that such reimaginings, if enacted, will fundamentally change the way we teach and learn. They will not. More importantly—they *have* not. The following examples are also lessons in humility, as both AI-zealots and AI-alarmists are consistently, and predictably, wrong when it comes to predicting what is possible, what will change, and what won't.

The Ancient Fear of Writing

We don't often think about it, but language and literacy are revolutionary human technologies (Hewes, 1993). Our invention of literacy has changed the course of history, enabled ideas to time travel and affect societies hundreds of years in the future. Literacy has also enriched our inner worlds by introducing us to the imaginings of others.

Right now, at this very moment, you are reading words that I first thought, then chose to write down. This is why I suggest that the process of writing and reading is a crude form of telepathy. These words do not capture one moment in time, since I have revised this section many times. In this way, these words on the page capture an amalgam of my thoughts over time, refined and rendered until I felt they were "good enough." You do not know what I am actually thinking, but I hope to have communicated the gist of it—all without you actually reading my mind.

Despite the affordances of literacy, (written) language is an imperfect technology with limitations. As Wittgenstein astutely mused in *Philosophical Investigations* (Wittgenstein, 2009/1953), the meanings of words are not fixed and instead are a set of interconnected meanings (i.e., "family resemblances"). Such meanings shift—both over time and based on who uttered them. I won't dive deep into the philosophy of language here, as the point is fairly intuitive. Slang, for example, gives everyone easy access to this concept. I still use "cool" to describe what I find interesting or pleasant, and I also use it to signal agreement. I also use "cool" to describe a pleasant ambient temperature. Readers who are a number of decades older than me, or younger than me, probably have a different set of meanings attached to the word, just as I have particular meanings attached to their own idiosyncratic use of words like "cook" (as in, let me cook) and "bet."

Human language, be it written or oral, is fascinating. Yet, up until fairly recently, many human beings had limited literacy skills, let alone advanced levels (Resnick & Resnick, 1966). Literacy as a human technology is powerful and responsible for much of our advancement. Historically, it is through reading the ideas of others that humanity has been able to ascend toward greater understanding of countless phenomena, from physics to biology to spirituality. In many cultures, the holiest artifacts in existence are words transcribed on the page by prophets inspired by their gods.

Written words are powerful, and up until a few years ago were squarely owned by humans (be they living or dead). That changed in 2022 when OpenAI created its first LLM. Yet, signals of this change predate the power of GenAI. All of the advancements related to LLMs and GenAI are predicated on written human language *at scale*. Without this, the synthetic language of GenAI would be impossible.

Through written words I am able to communicate my thoughts about AI's impact on education to an unseen audience that exists in my present, and extends an indeterminate amount of time into the future. Readers of this book are able to engage with how I think asynchronously. I have likely said something you disagree with, and that disagreement may have led to an . . . "unpleasant" thought about my scholarship. That's fine! Both because I cannot hear your thoughts as you read (thank god), and because my task is to engage you as a fellow thinker—regardless of whether or not you agree with me.

It is not an exaggeration to say that, without literacy, you and I would lead impoverished lives with limited understanding of our fellow human beings across space and time. We would simply *know* less, and the knowledge we did have would be a result of engaging with nearby family, friends, and acquaintances. Thus, our entire epistemology would be derived from the wisdom of those in close proximity to us. This world of decreased literacy is not necessarily a less human world, though I would argue that inhabiting such a world would prevent us from thoughtfully engaging with each other and the world around us.

I believe I've made my point; written language is great. Yet, Socrates, arguably one of the most influential philosophers of Western thought, was not a fan of it. Not only was he not a fan, he famously left none of his written works for us to examine. That task was left to his student Plato, another philosopher whose name you've likely heard, and who managed to write down what his mentor said. Socrates claimed that writing "will introduce forgetfulness" (Plato, c. 399–347 BCE, pp. 551–552). After all, if you write something down, why would you bother to remember it. Or, as Socrates put it: "[those who write] will not practice using their memory . . ." (Plato, c. 399–347 BCE, pp. 551–552).

Socrates's criticisms, however, went beyond the notion that writing would enable us to simply cheat our way out of using our memories. He argued that it would make people more ignorant over time:

> [Writing] will enable them to hear many things without being properly taught, and they will imagine that they have come to know much while for the most part they will know nothing.

This refrain of arguing that a technology will lead to the ruin of intelligence should feel eerily familiar. Read it again, with a more contemporary flair:

> [*GenAI*] will enable them to [*write*] many things without being properly taught, and they will imagine that they have come to know much while for the most part they will know nothing.

At its core, the argument against writing can be likened to the argument one hears from AI-alarmists, namely, that GenAI will lead to a sort of atrophy of human intelligence, such that many will think they know more than they do, without actually having a deep knowledge of any of it.

This argument is born from an impoverished understanding of how human beings integrate technology into their everyday lives. While it is true that GenAI *overuse* may lead to maladaptive outcomes, the core claim that it is *destined* to do so is incorrect for the same reasons Socrates was incorrect about writing, that is, human technology will be integrated and propel us in new directions.

Notice that I did not use "propel us forward" here, as it is an oversimplification to assume that all human technology leads toward some unidirectional "forward progress." Instead, our technology will merely cause us to act differently, and those differences may or may not be helpful to us (and our environments) in the long run.

Returning to Socrates, his disdain for writing was not predictive of a world where human memory ruled over and above what we write down. Instead, the world we live in, one where literacy rates are quite high relative to even a few hundred years ago (Altick, 1998; Sticht, 2002; Roser & Ortiz-Ospina, 2018), is a world rich with written expression *based* on human intelligence. In fact, as I argued at the start of this section, literacy has led to an explosion of innovation, rather than a sort of atrophy of our ability to think and reason. In fact, literacy is no longer seen as a "technology" in the popular imagination at all. It is a mundane fact of human existence.

Too Many Books!

Technological innovation can feel overwhelming, partially because we have difficulty parsing what it can do at first glance (a topic I cover at length in Chapter 4). The "newness" of technology has a tendency to tax our working memory because we have not integrated its functions into our everyday experiences. This "newness" can thus be a barrier that butts up against our desire to understand what is new. Consequently, it can be difficult to accommodate our behavior around a new technology, to integrate what's new so that it becomes useful. It isn't helpful that words and phrases like "innovation," "once in a generation," and "disruption" often accompany the launch of new technologies.

Some (or most) of this is marketing, as it is rare for a technology to be so foreign that it does not bear some resemblance to what came before. We also have a way of accommodating—indeed, acclimating—to changes so swiftly that new technologies often become relegated to the background in short order. (I do not think anyone is marveling over smartphones or touch screens anymore, for example.)

This is what I mean when I say that GenAI too will soon become mundane, if it hasn't already done so by the time this book hits the shelves. Such a thesis, however, is best served by further examining historical precedents. By juxtaposing the concerns of our peers a few hundred years (or so) removed, we can begin to see the edges of truth in my claim that GenAI tools will one day recede into the background of our everyday experiences.

This process, however, should be directed and we should understand how GenAI will get woven into our lives, so that we can recognize its use and not merely be subjected to automation that we have had little to no hand in creating or controlling. Enter Conrad Gessner (1516–1565), the "father" of bibliography (Bay, 1916). He was a Swiss physician and botanist with an ambitious goal: he wanted to itemize all the works written in Hebrew, Greek, and Latin up to that point in the 1500s.

Such an index (i.e., a bibliography) may not sound like an educational technology, or even an innovation, however we must always contextualize progress within the time it occurs. So to understand Gessner's contributions, we must imagine living during a time when "information overload" was defined as there being too many books out in circulation, when "too many" numbered in the thousands. Gessner lived in a world where written human language was largely confined to books (Socrates's nightmare) that were accessible to few individuals. To put that into context, contemporary estimates suggest that there are roughly 128 *million* books in circulation today (Giordano, 2023).

Gessner's work culminated in the *Bibleotheca univeralis* (Gessner, 1545). A work of both synthesis and documentation, Gessner could perhaps be considered one of the first applications of human intelligence that sought to understand all written knowledge. Unfortunately, Gessner's undertaking unveiled a problem. After cataloging over 3,000 books, Gessner determined that there were simply *too many* books:

> We have reason to fear that the multitude of books which grows every day in a prodigious fashion will make the following centuries fall into a state as barbarous as that of the centuries that followed the fall of the Roman Empire. Unless we try to prevent this danger by separating those books which we must throw out or leave in oblivion from those which one should save and within the latter between what is useful and what is not.

Not only were there simply too many books, the growth rate of books was destined to lead civilization toward ruin; not just *any* ruin, but a ruin that was likened to the fall of the Roman Empire. To Gessner, this unavoidable problem suggested a solution. Namely, the need to determine which books were valuable to avoid societal decline, and which were actually useful and should be preserved.

I sometimes wonder what Gessner would think about the current state of affairs, where written language is not relegated to published books and encompasses language on the internet. It's impossible to determine exactly how many human words exist online, but even a narrow analysis of one word (like sorting out whether or not the English word "people" is interpreted as male or female online) yields over 630 *billion* words (Smith, 2022). Gessner operated in simpler times, but his arguments nonetheless mirror our current concerns about the nature of information, GenAI, and how the two intersect in ways that will either threaten or enhance education in our world.

His analysis should also sound familiar in the age of GenAI and is even comparable to antiquity. A new technological trigger (in this case, books) yields an analysis that, on its face, sounds alarmist. Surely mere *thousands* of books should not be interpreted as a threat. Yet, we cannot wave away these concerns, as they are based on our own modern understanding of written language and its ubiquity in print and online. Still, there's something intriguing about a man who decided that his life's work was going to be to catalog all written knowledge and, in so doing, determined that there was simply too much of it.

Our task when it comes to interpreting the potential disruptive or innovative force of GenAI is to avoid the mistake of Gessner, and not be frightened by the vast amount of synthetic human language that can be generated, so much as to become AI-alarmists. Nor should we be blind to negative possibilities and become AI-zealots. Instead, we should be "temporally flexible," that is, we should situate our analysis of what's possible within multiple points in time; the past, where GenAI will seem like magic, the present where GenAI is disruptive, and the future where GenAI will be perfectly normal and a mundane part of human existence.

Television and the First "Artificial Teacher"

The notion that new technologies will disrupt, or otherwise affect students, teachers, and educational organizations is a persistent idea. New technologies have a way of urging us to rethink what's possible, both in negative and positive ways. The previous examples have examined this in ancient times and during the 1500s. Both examples focused on technologies related to language specifically. Both show that there was a time when the ubiquity of written language felt "new," and somewhat scary—an idea that feels ludicrous in today's world where written language is both easily accessible and seemingly never-ending. (That feeling is precisely the point I want you to linger on as you continue to read this book.)

Although the prevailing technologies have evolved over time in ways that are, quite literally, fantastic, our responses to them have followed similar patterns. The urge to see newer technologies (or their products, as is the case with books) as something to worry about is a predicament that we seem to find ourselves in often. For the remaining examples of this chapter, however, we'll stay squarely within the twentieth century, starting with post-secondary education during the 1950s in the United States.

A core issue in education during the late 1950s was contending with the scale that institutions needed to grow to accommodate returning soldiers interested in using the G.I. Bill to further their education. This challenge was compounded by the Baby Boom that followed soldiers' return from the Second World War and reintegration into society (Olson, 1973). The post-Second World War explosion of higher education, then, was partially a result of this process, and the discourse of the time gives us another inflection point to examine when considering how individuals in the past ruminated over new technology's impact on education.

The technology in question? The television. In *Must the TV Technicians Take over the College* Ernest Earnest (not a typo) opined on how television would come to make its mark on college campuses (Earnest, 1958):

> There is a note of panic in much of the discussion about mounting college enrollments. One might think that the prospect of twice the present college population ten years hence might seem good news to educators who have long deplored the cultural limitations of the American people. Instead, the almost unrelieved gloom of the prophets can only be matched by the prophesies of disaster at the time of the first G. I. Bill following World War II. Then, as now, the educational journals and the public prints were filled with discussions of the shortage of instructors, of the lack of facilities, and the baleful effects of overcrowding.

The premise of Earnest's writing will seem foreign to contemporary readers of this book, as there once was a time when the fears among educators focused on there being *too many* students. This would lead to issues we are familiar with, such as overcrowding and fewer resources to accommodate the influx of students. In today's world, the opposite problem is cause for concern. The "enrollment cliff" nears, and it is unclear how post-secondary institutions will cope with having fewer students to enroll (Schuette, 2023; Campion, 2020).

The solution of Earnest's day (i.e., using technology to solve staffing and overcrowding issues), however, should sound familiar. Indeed, despite the challenges of the 1950s being different from the issues we face in the 2020s, emerging technologies still played a role in how folks of the day sought solutions. Television was seen by some as a way to solve the challenges related to there being too many students, as Earnest's continues:

> In this atmosphere of alarm, all sorts of panaceas are being suggested by administrators and foundations. Americans tend to assume that any problem can be solved by a new pill, serum, or ingenious gadget. Thus, closed circuit television for the classroom has been seized upon as the most hopeful solution for the expected shortage of teachers. The Fund for the Advancement of Education has financed experiments with TV at several universities. At least 80 colleges are trying it out.

If we ignore Earnest's cheap shot at Americans (how rude!), we can see how a television, a newly ubiquitous technology in the 1950s, would make for a potential solution if we place it in the correct historical context. Lectures, or "direct instruction," were a common pedagogical strategy in post-secondary institutions in the 1950s. In fact, it's still exceedingly common now, however these days it's also possible to find more "constructivist" approaches to learning, where students take an active part in knowledge generation at the behest of their instructor (Fosnot, 2013; O'Connor, 2022).

Thus, if the problem is insufficient humans to do the job, surely a machine that broadcasts recorded humans will solve the issue! For anyone too young to remember what closed circuit television is, think of it as a private YouTube channel that is only accessible if you have the right credentials. The difference is that closed circuit TV wasn't on the internet (since there was no internet in the 1950s). Instead, the closed circuit was physical. So, in this way, colleges could have lectures broadcast on their own private networks for their students.

Despite the core differences in how TV and GenAI function, the role they play as technologies intended to solve a problem (imagined or otherwise) is eerily similar to one another. Earnest hints as much:

> The danger of educational TV is twofold. On the one hand, it may lead education into unexpected and undesirable channels; on the other, this seemingly easy solution of the teacher shortage may prevent a genuine re-examination of our system of higher education.

Earnest's brief discussion of the potential problems TV might cause is similar to the conversations we are having now about GenAI. It can lead us to strange places, and focusing on the impact of the technology prevents us from having more important conversations—like treating students as customers who buy credentials rather than citizens who need a broad range of skills to contribute to society.

The current discourse is (unfortunately) too similar to previous discourses brought on by different technological triggers. Patterns in how technology might influence, disrupt, or otherwise interact with education myopically focus on the technology rather than the humans who use it. It's important to remember, however, that the alarm—and overstated potential—of a new technology follows the same pattern. In the 1950s, television was viewed as a revolutionary technology that could potentially replace teachers in classrooms. It didn't. I suspect the same will be true of GenAI.

The 1:1 Device Program and Myth of Productivity

We are not always suspicious of new technologies, however. Often zealotry takes center stage instead, and decisions are made to deploy new technologies in schools as fast as possible—often without first considering the context where they will be deployed. I linger on this point in the next chapter, but for now let's briefly examine how excitement and optimism can lead us astray just as quickly as skepticism.

The good news is that we do not have to travel that far back in time to discover the consequences of zealotry. Roughly a decade ago there were many conversations and debates about "revolutionizing" education by giving every student access to a device, be it a tablet or a laptop. For the most part, those on the side of rapidly deploying new technologies won the debate, and the notion of ensuring 1:1 (one laptop for every student) was popularized.

To that end, there were many initiatives across the globe determined to give every student access to the latest personal and portable electronic device. Los Angeles Unified School District (LAUSD), for example, began rolling out iPads in 2013 at the cost of roughly $1.3 billion dollars

(Lapowsky, 2015). The excitement for iPads was widespread and included smaller districts as well as schools globally (McCrea, 2010; Grannell, 2010). All of these initiatives were well intentioned. As computational power became more portable, this enabled technology to be personal. It was no longer necessary to have a large desktop computer in the back of the classroom or entire computer labs devoted to giving students access to new learning software. On the face of it, the push for 1:1 initiatives makes sense, but *execution* matters.

It is unsurprising, then, that the rollout of these initiatives was uneven, and sometimes disastrous. LAUSD is a famous example of 1:1 initiatives ending poorly, with a turbulent rollout that included students hacking devices to enable them to be used for more general purposes (Pickert, 2014). Events compounded from there, eventually leading officials to seek refunds due to what they considered unacceptable software—though an investigation later revealed shortcuts to what should have been a competitive bidding process that led to the resignation of LAUSD's superintendent John Deasy (Pickert, 2014; Lapowsky, 2015).

Thus optimism gave way to uneven—or disastrous—rollouts of educational technologies. This is because devices, be they laptops or tablets, are merely tools, and as such they must integrate harmoniously within the learning environments they are meant to be deployed in. This includes ensuring that those who would use them have the training to know their affordances and limitations.

This is why the science is mixed on 1:1 programs. Work that has studied the deployment of devices to every student has shown null results (e.g., Bixler 2019; Carr, 2012) as well as positive results (e.g., Al-Mashaqbeh, 2016; Kirkpatrick et al., 2018). This shouldn't be surprising, as variability in outcomes is common with the introduction of new technologies into the classroom. Thus it would be incorrect to conclude that iPads, tablets, and the like were utter failures when it came to producing positive effects on students' academic achievement.

In fact, meta-analytic work suggests the opposite; after analyzing 20 studies with over 2,800 participants, Aspiranti and Larwin (2021) show that there were statistically significant math gains when tablet-based interventions were used in the classroom. These are positive results, yet the authors also found differences based on the socioeconomic status (SES) of students, where those from higher SES had larger positive effects. Overall, the positive effects of tablets can be demonstrated in aggregate, but it bears in mind that every success is a *localized* success based on how a device is used. Indeed, both Aspiranti and Larwin (2021) suggest as much in their discussion, concluding that:

> Significant differences in the effects of using a specific app versus not using a specific app demonstrate the importance of explicitly choosing an app to use during an intervention and not simply allowing the tablet itself to be an intervention.

In the end, the evidence is clear: adoption of 1:1 device programs (e.g., laptops and iPads) does not guarantee academic gains, technology is contextual and requires harmony among users, the learning environment, and the technology itself. We must therefore examine all aspects of the local context to understand and potentially predict the results of including additional technologies. We turn to this task in the next chapter.

3

EdTech "Reimagines" Education

Chapter Outline

Introduction

Chapter 2 suggested that we aren't very good at predicting how technologies interact with the educational systems we have come to rely on. This is, for better or worse, a fundamental part of who we are. We imagine utopias and dystopias resulting from inflection points based on our technological progress and tend to be incorrect. Yet, that doesn't stop us from trying, be it for altruistic or opportunistic reasons.

Currently, we are in the midst of thinking about how GenAI technologies will reshape education. Our thoughts range from AI-zealotry to AI-alarmism, and encompass everything in between. What's important to note, however, is that in the current age of AI "disruption" (or "opportunity") there have been calls to see how GenAI will "reimagine" education (e.g., Easley, 2025; Garner, 2025; Kubulan, 2025).

I find such calls perplexing. Not because they are fundamentally incorrect—I think it is perfectly fine to push ourselves to think about the consequences of integrating GenAI into different educational contexts. Instead, I find it perplexing because such calls to reimagine education come less than a decade after *other* calls to reimagine education. I'm not even sure we've finished the first set of "reimaginings," so it is strange to start another series of the same conversations.

Less than a decade ago, during the pandemic, there were calls to reimagine how education might be different post-pandemic. Such calls seemed to follow public and private investments that enabled formal education to limp along during imposed quarantines (e.g., Bryant et al., 2020). Looking back, it is unavoidable to consider how calls for reimagining education came at the heels of pandemic-induced calamity.

I will not revisit the pandemic at length, or comment on how the United States responded to the need to protect its citizens from COVID-19. States reacted differently (Hallas et al., 2021; Halloran et al., 2021), and students had differing experiences based on entirely predictable variables, like socioeconomic status. What seems true, regardless of politics, is that students suffered mentally and academically (Correa & First, 2021; Cohodes et al., 2022). Whether or not we call that "learning loss" (Engzell et al., 2021; Polikoff & Silver, 2022) is irrelevant. What seems unarguable is that some of the negative educational consequences from the pandemic were unavoidable, whereas other negative consequences were mitigated by investment in schools (Weber & Baker, 2025).

The initial rhetoric during the early days of the pandemic advocated for a new world where education could be "reimagined" or "revolutionized" with the help of educational technologies. Unsurprisingly, this did not occur—but why? This chapter answers this question by introducing the concept of the "sociotechnical system" (Cooper & Foster, 1971; Rizzo et al., 2000; Wilson, 2000; Carayon, 2006).

Up to now I have discussed technologies as entities that act apart from us, yet, the truth of the matter is that technologies are *embedded* in our everyday lives in important ways. They interact with people, places, and other technologies. This is the core idea behind the sociotechnical system. It is a way to examine how technologies seamlessly integrate into our everyday lives, enabling us to do work that is more efficient and work that expresses our values. The system is "socio" because it embeds societal norms and actions that we must surface in order to understand technology's place in educational settings. It is a "system" because it is a set of interactions between distinct entities.

Throughout this chapter I will define and expand on the three pillars of the sociotechnical system: (1) The User, (2) The Technology, and (3) The Social Context. When technology "just works" we can presume that there is harmony among the three different pillars of the sociotechnical system. When it doesn't, one of our first diagnostic steps should be to examine which pillar of the sociotechnical system is in disharmony, because without harmony among the three pillars, any new technology—no matter how revolutionary—is not positioned to live up to its potential. Worse, it might actually be positioned to do more harm than good.

I will expand on these ideas by discussing the pandemic and schools' response to the necessity to move to remote learning modalities. I choose this example for a few reasons. First, the pandemic is proximal; it didn't occur that long ago and thus we likely remember it. Second, the pandemic and its effects were ubiquitous. Everyone, globally, had to deal with policies and decisions that were predicated on the pandemic. Finally, it is a good example of what happens when the sociotechnical system works, and when it doesn't. The research I will draw on (much of it my own) illustrates the negative consequences of a disharmonious sociotechnical system, as well as what happens when folks rally and "make it work."

By using the pandemic as a starting point, Chapter 3 applies the notion of the sociotechnical system to emerging GenAI educational technologies. I argue that without fully understanding the role that people play and the training necessary to leverage the potential of GenAI, that GenAI itself will not be nearly as revolutionary as many presume it will be.

The Sociotechnical System

If you have ever been involved with handling logistics for an event, no matter how small, then you know how important it is to create a "frictionless" experience for those who attend. Good logistics are invisible and enable others to work to their full potential. When I was the Director of Institute Technology at Teach For America's summer institute over a decade ago, I was tasked with creating such experiences for TFA corps members who needed to write lesson plans, print handouts, and do everything expected of new teachers. This required giving them access to a working computer lab, printers, and other technology they could use without it "getting in the way."

I'm certain that you can think about a time in your life when you were in charge of creating a similar environment. It doesn't need to be as involved as a computer lab. Organizing a dinner party also requires forethought and knowing which technologies you will deploy to curate a successful evening. Do you bake dinner, or cook it on the stovetop? How will you keep it warm as guests arrive? Where will the dirty dishes go? Technology plays a role in answering all of those questions, though we often do not think of it that way.

Thus, the scale of the event doesn't matter. The core idea is creating circumstances that enable individuals to act freely and feel a sense of agency in doing so, while minimizing disruptions. In education, this facilitates the potential for "flow states" to emerge (Csikszentmihalyi et al., 2014). Such states are incredibly helpful because when everything works, everyone is engaged, and things get done. When this happens in the classroom, students learn.

This notion of creating such spaces lies at the core of the "sociotechnical system." When *things* work, *people* can work, and when people work, things get done. This requires people, technologies, and their intersection (people using technologies) to be in harmony. As I've already mentioned, the sociotechnical system is composed of three parts: people, technologies, and contexts.

My favorite example to demonstrate how the sociotechnical system works is driving a car. (And not because I'm from California.) If you have ever driven a car, as I assume many of you have, then you know it requires (at least) three elements. A driver, a car, and a road. The experience of driving is based on these three elements working *in harmony*. If you are a passenger in a car when a sixteen-year-old learns how to drive, for example, then it really doesn't matter how good the car is or what road you're on—it's going to be a rough (exciting?) ride. Similarly, a Formula 1 race car driver will not be able to overcome bad roads while driving a clunker of a car. Both of the above examples represent a dissonant sociotechnical system.

If we take this analogy and apply it to educational technologies in general, or GenAI in particular, we begin to see how essential it is for the sociotechnical system to work well. Students, teachers, and others need to know how to *use* educational technologies powered by GenAI. The GenAI technologies themselves need to be functional and useful, with a set of capabilities that can help students learn or teachers teach. Further, schools—or other learning environments—need to be designed to support both the people and the technologies. A classroom without working internet, for example, would be a context that disabled, rather than enabled, the use of GenAI technologies.

Without harmony within the sociotechnical system, the overall experience is at minimum impoverished, and at maximum it can exacerbate existing disparities. Try to imagine the sociotechnical system as a three-legged stool; if one of the legs is compromised, then the entire stool wobbles and becomes unstable. Thus, the user, the technology itself, and the broader social context all need to be sturdy enough to bear the weight of use. A stool with two strong legs and one rotten one will still be useless for the person who wishes to sit. Similarly, we can still sit on a wobbly stool—it's not catastrophic—but our experience is impoverished if we're constantly minding our balance due to the wobble.

Pandemic-Era Calls for Reimagining Education

The sociotechnical system is not merely an abstraction. In fact, I wager that all of us have experienced recent failures when it comes to technologies operating in harmony with people and contexts. The most recent (and likely salient) case of this is the COVID-19 pandemic, and the havoc it wreaked on public schooling.

A disclaimer: I will bracket debates about the necessity for remote learning, I am not a public health expert nor a virologist. I am a scholar of educational technologies, and whether we like it or not, remote learning was imposed as a measure to keep us from catching COVID-19 and subsequent variants. This led to different consequences among different communities. Thus, I focus on the fact that during the pandemic, schools moved toward remote instruction. When they did so, and for how long, varied among districts and states (Leech et al., 2022).

The shift from in-person instruction to remote instruction was abrupt, occurring around late March 2020 (CDC, 2024). I recall getting an email from my university stating that all instruction would happen remotely, so I drove to campus, picked up essentials, and did not return for over a year. I did not have much time to plan. No one did.

As a result, many school districts were not prepared for what it meant to move to a remote system of instruction (e.g., Richmond, 2020). Returning to my car analogy from earlier, all educators were asked to go "off road" with the car they happened to be driving at the time. So were students. This led to different approaches based on different capabilities and institutional capacities to support remote instruction. I had no illusions that pandemic-era remote instruction would go well. Teaching is hard. Teaching under the duress imposed by external factors that cause one to completely alter the learning environment is *harder*.

I imagine that most educators on the front lines felt similarly, which is why I was surprised to witness discourse focused on "reimagining" or "revolutionizing" education *during the pandemic*. To me, that felt like hiring a designer and a contractor to renovate your home while it's still on fire. (Maybe let's put out the fire and assess what was damaged first?)

That may read as very "hindsight is 20/20" to some, but let's examine, for a moment, the actual discourse of the time:

> [Arne] Duncan said the current crisis should be an opportunity to fundamentally rethink everything: "There's no better time to do that than now" . . . In another GSV Ventures [Superintendent Tom] Rooney said educators are realizing that many more students than they previously thought can handle self-directed or online learning. (Mathewson, 2020)
>
> [B]eing forced to adapt to distance learning means that schools such as Essex Tech have a chance to reimagine how CTE is taught . . . "[n]ecessity does breed invention, and this situation we're all facing certainly qualifies

> as necessity," Robin Lake, the director of the Center on Reinventing Public Education at the University of Washington (Richmond, 2020)
>
> Now is the time to chart a vision for how education can emerge stronger from this global crisis than ever before and propose a path for capitalizing on education's newfound support in virtually every community across the globe. (Vegas & Winthrop, 2020)
>
> The pandemic has changed us. It forced our nation to adapt . . . [r]ight now, an enormous opportunity exists to transform education. (Biden, 2021)

There are many more examples of leaders, educators, innovators, and even lay people suggesting that pandemic-era remote learning was a perfectly reasonable time to reimagine education. Some opinions were tempered, others were naive, and others were grandiose and unrealistic. Drastic systemic change has a way to force reflection. Yet, reflection and planning for innovation and "reimagining" without attending to the sociotechnical system was doomed to fail.

The Dream of Reimagining Turns into a Nightmare

I am not a pessimist by nature; I am a pragmatist who tries to plan for hardship so that I can mitigate its effects while taking advantage of potential opportunities that reveal themselves. That is why the discourse around reimagining education (or reinventing it) felt out of place during 2020 and 2021. While the pandemic was indeed a catalyst for change, that is not the same as being a catalyst for *positive* change in education when the reality on the ground was much different.

The reality was that while well-intentioned, calls to remake education also highlighted deep digital inequities among students. For example, many students, particularly those from low-income or rural backgrounds, lacked access to reliable internet or the necessary technology to participate fully in online learning environments (Aguilar et al., 2022; Graves et al., 2021). This lack of access—the digital equity gap—led to persistent learning loss that we are still recovering from today. This series of events was *absolutely* predictable, especially if one understands that (educational) technologies must work in harmony with the environment and the people who use them. This is the essence of the sociotechnical system.

It is worthwhile to interrogate the events of remote learning through the sociotechnical lens. To that end, regardless of internal expertise, resources, and knowledge among students and parents; everyone went remote. This was a fundamental shift in one of the three pillars: the educational environment, that is, the road in our driving analogy.

Yet, a change in one part of the system affects others. Teachers had to learn how to use new technologies that enabled remote instruction (i.e., the "driver" in our analogy), and the tools themselves were rapidly developed or changed (i.e., the car in our analogy). Zoom, for example, was not ubiquitous *until* the pandemic (Isaacs et al., 2020; Karl et al., 2022). This rapid deployment of unfamiliar educational technologies led to the quick development of resources to help others learn how to use them. Research on immediate impacts of their use also ramped up.

My work of the time, for example, sought to provide a way to think about technologies that could be adapted to remote learning through the lens of "technology stewardship," (Aguilar, 2020a), which required teachers and administrators to understand the affordances of the technologies they chose to deploy. I similarly created guidelines to help teachers think creatively about how to ensure that not all instruction was based on the use of technology that some students didn't have access to (Aguilar, 2020b).

There were many such responses from the academic community that aimed to help everyone "skill up" and respond to the imperatives of imposed remote instruction. There were gaps in expertise that needed to be filled; importantly, there was also no set definition of what "remote" meant from a pedagogical perspective. "Remote" could mean, for example, *synchronous* instruction, where a teacher leads class via a video conferencing software like Zoom. It could also mean *asynchronous* instruction, where a teacher assigns work for students to be completed at their own pace.

These approaches are not equal. Work in this area has shown that learning outcomes can be improved with synchronous activities that enhance students' perception of connectedness with teachers and peers (Shin, 2003). Asynchronous feedback, moreover, is also difficult to get right; if students get less feedback, they tend to not do as well and can also lose their motivation to persist.

Limited contact with peers also has negative effects (Galusha, 1997). Unstructured learning where students might "discover" is not as beneficial as learning that is guided by an expert teacher. This includes things like feedback, worked examples, and scaffolding. All of these net positive pedagogical approaches require live instruction.

Whether you were a parent, student, or teacher, one common thread was that initial responses to the pandemic were chaotic. Many districts responded well, while others struggled. There was also an infusion of resources at the federal level through ESSER funds, which helped plug resource holes. Regardless of the school and system, however, the pandemic serves as a useful case study in how educational technologies must exist with support from users and learning environments.

As I mentioned at the beginning of this chapter, one of the first things that happened during the pandemic was hope. There were calls to reimagine, revolutionize, or otherwise rethink what education *could be*. Looking back, it is easy to think these thoughts were naive. Everyone was trying to get by, survive a deadly virus, and find a sense of normalcy. Why, then, would we bother to take the time to *also* reimagine an education system that was limping along, trying to adapt to circumstances it was not built for? Calls to reimagine or reinvent education as GenAI tools continue to proliferate feel similar to what happened during the pandemic. Such approaches may have some potential, but we should still take a careful and pragmatic approach, rather than be ruled by the whims of AI-zealots or AI-alarmists.

Failure Without Sociotechnical Harmony

In retrospect, it is easy to see why many were seduced by the potential for positive impacts of remote learning on students. The decade prior to the pandemic, work that examined blended learning found positive effects when courses had online modalities (e.g., Means et al., 2013). Yet, it was naive to treat remote learning during a global pandemic as fertile ground to replicate those positive outcomes.

The pandemic was hard, and it showed us what happens when systems that have been in place for decades are disrupted by global events. We were forced to create stop-gap measures to ensure a semblance of continuity. It was a mistake to treat such stop-gap measures as opportunities to "innovate," or the means to "reimagine" the system. Reimagining a system that is on the brink of collapse is at best irresponsible, and at worst depraved. That likely reads as harsh, but the truth of the matter is that people who wish to reimagine systems are often the same as those who are insulated from the effects of experimentation. When the stakes are all "academic," it is easy to tinker with systems that affect the education and livelihoods of others.

The effects of the pandemic on education were massive. Major disruptions to traditional educational models forced educators, students, and policymakers to rethink how education needed to change to be delivered at scale. This resulted in many models with differing impacts on students. Internationally, for example, Lichand, Dória, and colleagues (2021) found that remote instruction led to an over 300 percent dropout rate. These findings were mirrored by work in the United States that showed an increase in dropout rates for students in the United States (e.g., Dorn et al., 2020; Moscoviz & Evans, 2022) that further led to learning loss among more vulnerable groups (e.g., Moscoviz & Evans, 2022; Polikoff & Silver, 2022). Effects also differed based on socioeconomic status, with students with lower SES generally doing poorly compared to their high SES peers (e.g., Chen, 2024).

It is no surprise then, that "[on] average, the learning progress of school-aged children . . . slowed substantially during the pandemic," resulting in roughly "35% of a school year's worth of learning" (Betthäuser et al., 2023). These shifts were dynamic, however, with more recent work indicating that some ground was made up later in the pandemic with "course failures, and grade retention [rebounding] . . . toward prepandemic levels, but absences [worsening]" (Fuller et al., 2025).

Given this evidence of struggle, it seems almost silly to remember that during the disruption, there were calls to "remake" or "reimagine" education. Many of these calls were based on the idea that technology used during the pandemic could scale and make education more accessible for all. Such predictions proved to be overly optimistic.

I do not recount these negative effects to place blame. Instead, I use them to highlight the fact that despite our best efforts, with the best technologies available to us at the time, failures occurred because solutions cannot be driven by technology. Instead, they must be driven by people who happen to *use* technology, and their use of technology must work with the other factors of the sociotechnical system. In short, when we only think of technology and not how it integrates into the educational ecosystem, we invite failure. The roles of teachers, students, and the social context must be fully accounted for in order for solutions to have a higher likelihood of success.

The Sociotechnical System and GenAI

Examining change through the lens of the sociotechnical system will enable you to conduct some thought experiments that will, in turn, help you to think about GenAI's potential impact on education. It is my hope that doing this will demonstrate that GenAI need not be a fantastic revolutionary tool as defined by AI-zealots, nor does it need to be a threat as defined by an AI-alarmists.

Instead, the best way to think about GenAI is as a set of tools that need to be *integrated* into the everyday practices of educators and learners alike. But first, I underscore the fact that GenAI use in education will not reach its full potential unless we address the human element. Doing so will ensure that users are well-trained and the technology fits seamlessly into the educational environment. This will require educators at all levels to not ignore GenAI development. While not everyone needs to become an expert, nearly everyone should possess a familiarity regarding the affordances and limitations of GenAI technologies.

The user, the technology, and the context where both operate. These are the three pieces of the sociotechnical system. They can be applied to any technology one thinks of, as I have shown in the preceding pages—but what about GenAI and education? This is where things can get a little tricky, beginning with thinking of GenAI as a single "technology."

Rather than think of GenAI as a unified technology with a singular purpose, it is important to decompose it into its constituent parts. Doing this conceptual work allows us to meaningfully interrogate the capabilities of a particular GenAI tool. To this end, GenAI technologies can be best likened to a constellation of stars. They are related bodies that can act similarly, and they are *patterned* while inhabiting similar space.

This metaphor lets us do a few things. First, we can examine each tool by itself (the "star"). Second, we can understand the larger pattern that is formed by related tools (the "constellation"). Finally, we can begin to examine larger patterns, and how they fit into our environment, much like how astronomers understand one constellation in relation to others in the night sky.

GenAI applications are built on top of "foundation models" that can be understood as the engine that powers the rest of the application (Brown et al., 2020; Radford et al., 2019). OpenAI's GPT large language model (LLM) is an example of a foundation model. For our purposes, we can consider it the basic building block that enables the technology to function. Each version brings more capabilities (e.g., version 3.5 vs. version 5 models). Regardless of the new capabilities different versions provide the user, foundation models are, by definition, dependent on the data used to train them.

What makes LLMs and tools like ChatGPT, Gemini, and so on, so powerful is that they are trained on *vast* amounts of data, the analysis of which is computationally intensive (Kaplan et al., 2020). That is why large data centers are needed to make them function. Without computational power, all we have is data, not a product or a service. The large data sets, and the computational power used to process them, are why conversations with GenAI chatbots feel like conversations with actual non-human intelligences. Their answers to our questions are simply fast predictions of language that "sounds about right" given our query.

There is much more to say when to comes to foundation models and how they shift what products built on top of them can do, but it isn't necessary to dive into those technical explanations as we examine the sociotechnical system vis-à-vis GenAI. To that end, for you to apply the concept of the sociotechnical system to educational practice, it is helpful to think of two potential case studies.

- Case A: ChatGPT Paid version that is used by an average 18-year-old college student in a required introductory writing course. Their instructor banned the use of AI. The student is unfamiliar with how GenAI technologies work but is comfortable engaging with chatbots.
- Case B: Magic School AI that is used by a mid-career middle school teacher who teaches in a school district generally supportive of AI. The district has limited expertise with AI and is sensitive to legal liability. The teacher is known to be the "technology steward" of the

> school, and many go to them for tech help. Midway through the year, the school bans all AI, however, leading the teacher to use it on their personal machine.

Now that you have an idea of two potential use-cases, I will list the relevant components of the sociotechnical system, that is, technology, user, and context. For Case A, we know that the paid version of ChatGPT is generally more capable than the free version, which suggests that the student may use it more often. They will also have access to more sophisticated features. Yet, the student may not know how to use all of these features, since they are a novice user.

GenAI hallucinations might slip their attention, for example. Moreover, using GenAI in this setting might be risky, since their instructor has a clear bias against the technology. There are countless permutations of what could happen to the student in Case A. They could be correctly accused of academic dishonesty—they could also be unjustly accused. They could use GenAI for instrumental help-seeking, which would help them master material better, or they could use it for executive help seeking and simply use GenAI as an "answer" machine (Macias & Aguilar, 2026).

For Case B we can follow a similar train of thought. An expert teacher that others use as a resource is more likely to do innovative things, but only within the realm of possibilities defined by the other aspects of the sociotechnical system. What started as a year of innovation (e.g., using Magic School to create personalized worksheets, lesson plans, etc.) might be stymied once the school decides to ban all use of AI, or otherwise limit its use in order to address parental concerns about AI. Administrators in the school could also wish to return to the "basics."

As with Case A, the details matter and we cannot simply say that GenAI use is "good" or "bad" until we understand the broader context. Thus, we cannot even begin to understand possibilities without more details than what I've given you.

I invite you to sit with both cases for a while and think of possibilities that are all based on each aspect of the sociotechnical system. It might also be useful to find other real-world examples drawn from your personal or professional experiences. In so doing, you will see that there are no *general* answers to proper use, and instead, answers are based on details that have to be fleshed out. This is something that should be done in each educational setting in order to ensure positive uses of GenAI technologies.

Training and the Human Element: Preparing for AI Integration

While every aspect of the sociotechnical system in education is important, not all of it is under our direct control at any given time. For example, it is quite often that we cannot change the learning environment we find ourselves in. Nor do we always have the resources to buy the latest generation educational technologies. More often than not, technologies and learning environments are imposed on us. That is why it is important to focus on the user. Thus, it is vitally important to properly train educators, students, and administrators to use GenAI technologies effectively. Failure to provide this training will prevent GenAI from achieving the positive outcomes often promised and might contribute to misuse and/or overuse.

Given the rapid pace that GenAI technologies evolve, it would be a mistake in my view to focus on specific uses of specific technologies, as there is a high likelihood that such advice would be incorrect within months of this book's publication. Instead, it is pragmatic to take a slightly abstract approach that can shape the way you *think* about GenAI tools.

Harkening back to earlier in this chapter, I am not interested in describing particular stars in the sky, I am interested in helping you learn how to detect constellations so that you can better attend to larger patterns of use that will (usually) prove true regardless of the GenAI technology you encounter. (If the stars analogy doesn't work for you, don't worry, that's the last you'll read of it.)

We now know that the user, the technology, and the context matter. Whether or not GenAI fails or succeeds depends on how all three of these elements work together. How then, might we begin to *integrate* GenAI into our practices? First, we must jettison the notion that current generation GenAI tools are *intelligent*. They are not. They are sophisticated, complex, and innovative, but they are not intelligent agents that deserve to be thought of as pseudo-human.

Thus, it is useful to not think of GenAI as "artificial intelligence" at all, and instead think of GenAI tools by focusing on the "generative" aspect that defines their function. To better understand how to integrate GenAI into education, we ought to think of *all* GenAI tools that focus on language (i.e., LLMs) as "Synthetic Human Language Machines," or SHLMs if you desperately need an acronym.

Many readers at this point may roll their eyes; "here is another academic who wants to split hairs and introduce a new term while doing it." Those readers are correct! However, some hairs need splitting—especially matted ones, to torture the metaphor. I have hopefully convinced you by now that language is a powerful human invention because it carries *meaning*. Language is how we understand each other and the phenomena around us.

"Synthetic Human Language Machine," then, communicates some key concepts. The first word signals my intention. Things that are *synthetic*, are not naturally occurring phenomena. They are human creations. Synthetic, moreover, is not an inherently negative term. I use synthetic brushes when I paint miniatures, as they are stiffer and can make detail work easier. They are also cheaper and more disposable compared to my natural Kolinsky Sable brushes. Why? Because Kolinsky brushes require the harvesting of fur from the Kolinsky Sable (which is more of a weasel, but that's beside the point).

In GenAI's case, the human language that is generated is "synthetic" because the words produced are not naturally occurring—humans didn't write them. That does not mean that it is not *useful* language. It is! But we must begin to see the language as synthetic *first* before we can assign value to the language. Once we do that, we can linger on the final word in the term: machine.

GenAIs that use LLMs are, at their core, synthetic human language *machines*. Thought of in this way we can begin to decouple GenAI from "intelligence" in all the ways that matter. GenAI tools do not *think*—they *generate* (Bender & Koller, 2020). Much like a factory machine can generate parts, GenAI machines generate words. These words can be useful, or they can be useless. Just like the output from factory machines we can also begin to think of "tolerances," that is, how much error we are willing to live with when we are working with the machine. We can also think of quality assurance procedures to make sure that the synthetic language that is generated is both useful and correct.

We can further broaden this definition to "Synthetic Human Artifact Machines" (SHAMs) if we wish to discuss other human artifacts, such as AI-generated music, images, video, voice, and so on. I note that "SHAM" is not antagonistic on purpose—it is merely a delightful accident. It turns out that human-written language can be serendipitous rather than hallucinatory.

Thought of in this way, GenAI technologies are perfectly fine and can be integrated into many educational spaces. The fact that the language—or artifacts—GenAI produces is synthetic is consequential but not inherently negative. Few would, for example, criticize a musician for using a synthesizer or other instruments that mimic analog instruments and/or tones.

Going back to my earlier point, both my Kolinsky brushes and my synthetic brushes serve their purpose, and those purposes are different. I do not confuse one purpose for the other despite the fact that they look *very* similar and *could* be used interchangeably. If I did use them interchangeably or act as though they were identical, then I would simply be applying a crude understanding of what their artistic affordances are to the task at hand.

Similarly, if someone asserts that GenAI, as a synthetic human language machine, can *replace* an expert, then we can begin to question their understanding of what experts are. Expertise, after all, is not simply a matter of generating language to answer a question, it is to anticipate unasked questions, to interrogate possible answers, to make unlikely connections, and to operate at the edges of a domain. The current state of GenAI cannot do any of those things reliably.

Make no mistake, I do not think that "SHLM" will catch on as a new term that many will use, let alone adopt. In truth, "GenAI" and "AI" are both terms that are more monetizable. Those terms create hype, which is tightly coupled with the potential monetary value that is of great interest to the tech industry and the venture capitalists that invest in it. That is why Sam Altman invokes a possible world where ChatGPT iterations will enable folks to have a team of "experts" in their pocket (Yang & Cui, 2025). That conceptualization of GenAI is, after all, much more enticing than having a "Synthetic Human Language Generator" or "Synthetic Human Artifact Machine" in one's pocket. Yet, both latter terms are more accurate definitions of what is currently possible.

This rhetorical move can serve as a premise for creating training modules for educators and professionals alike. What synthetic element is being generated, and why is it useful? This enables us to think of what is generated in relation to the users of the generated synthetic content.

It encourages us to think of users based on their role (students, teachers, administrators), and then layer on additional dimensions as needed. For example, we can think of a student who is relatively inexperienced with technology and further refine a potential use-case for GenAI by thinking of a student who is a novice technology user and also not a strong writer. Those three dimensions (of many) enable us to begin to understand how they might use GenAI tools and generated artifacts.

Beyond Technology Alone

The third dimension of the sociotechnical system is complex and dynamic; it requires us to ask many follow-up questions. For example, suppose a student is using GenAI to help them study or to help them complete an assignment. Potential questions include: For which class and for what subject? What are the institutional policies at play, and how are those policies enacted within the classroom? We pose the first question because we know that both educators and academic subjects have different sensibilities when it comes to the use of GenAI. The student may be working on an assignment for a class that uses technology (e.g., computer science), but they may be instructed by an educator who does not believe GenAI should be used by students and has consequently banned its use. If so, the educator may be in alignment *or* in conflict with the policies that the larger institution has in place—or even the departmental versions of those policies.

Still, thought experiments only go so far when it comes to preparing for a future where GenAI will impose itself on both innocuous and important dimensions of education. We can imagine a user and a technology well enough, but contexts have a way of shifting and evolving in ways that are unpredictable. That is why hypotheticals of students' GenAI use do not always capture important nuances that are the result of other factors. These can include the educational institution, the student's instructor, the student's peers, and other factors that all influence (either directly or indirectly) the educational experience of our imagined student.

This is why it is difficult to say what the impact of GenAI will be on students and institutions long term. We are in the middle of an acclimation process where practices that use GenAI are varied in both complexity and efficacy. This acclimation process is a result of three intertwined dimensions: (1) the user, (2) the actual technology, and (3) the environment where the technology is used.

We don't often think about those distinctions unless something goes wrong. If I watch TV, I just watch TV. I don't need to think about turning it on, finding a show, the electricity that makes it work, or even the network and team of creatives that made the show happen. It is fully integrated into my environment. It's only when something goes wrong that I begin to "notice" the act of watching TV. The same is true for GenAI, and literally every other technology you use every day. Take a moment and think about the tech you use. When do you notice it? When do you simply use it? Why does that matter?

The current moment feels tumultuous because we do not have mental schema or organizational policies to lean on. This is why GenAI has disrupted the status quo. This disruption, however, is not the same as "innovation," as the base of evidence to make that claim must develop over time. In the meantime, the goal of this chapter was to push you to think beyond GenAI. People and social contexts matter just as much as technology. Without recognizing the importance of these elements, GenAI will remain an underutilized—or misused—tool rather than a force for meaningful change.

4

The Role of Design Affordances

Chapter Outline

Introduction

Tools are everywhere, and it's important for us to understand them. In this chapter, I explore the concept of "perceived affordances," drawing from Don Norman's (2013) work on design and Martin Heidegger's (1962) notions about why tool use matters when studying the human condition. Both scholars can contribute to our understanding of GenAI.

Norman's ideas enable us to examine designed objects to understand how their designs suggest potential uses. Heidegger, on the other hand, makes a broader point: that what it means to be human, and how to enact our "human-ness" can be explored through the tools we design and use. In discussing Heidegger I'll linger on his concepts of "ready-to-hand" and "present-at-hand."

Though written decades, oceans, and languages apart, Norman's and Heidegger's ideas are critical tools to understand the implications of GenAI on education. Norman's ideas about design affordances help us see what technology is trying to communicate. Heidegger, on the other hand, reminds us that the way we use technologies shapes who we are in profound ways, that is, how we interact with tools and technologies influences our very sense of being.

Together, these ideas help us better understand what GenAI tools have to offer educators, students, and parents. Norman's and Heidegger's ideas further serve to protect us against the polemics forwarded by both AI-zealots and AI-alarmists. Thus, Norman and Heidegger enable us to move beyond hype and fear, and toward understanding GenAI as a tool to be used.

Both scholars give us the mental tools to examine what GenAI tools can do, and what they cannot do. Their ideas will further enable us to engage with GenAI with confidence. Educators, for their part, can use the ideas proposed by Norman and Heidegger to vet AI applications in education without being seduced by empty promises propagated by EdTech startups. Educators can further avoid the fear mongering that serves as fuel for the consulting careers of opportunistic GenAI naysayers.

The chapter ends with an emphasis on the book's core thesis: our discussions related to GenAI in education must be a balanced discussion that centers on both incredible possibilities and clear limitations. Ultimately, I emphasize that we shouldn't become enamored with tools to the point of ignoring their limitations. By understanding both what GenAI is designed to do and what it cannot achieve, we can ensure that we use it in a way that truly benefits educators and students.

Norman's Perceived Affordances

Have you ever picked up an unfamiliar object or tool, and deduced how it could be used? It doesn't have to be a complex tool—even the pastime of picking up a good stick and swinging it enables you to evaluate its potential "affordances," that is, how it could be used. The difference between a stick and a *designed* tool, however, is that designed tools have built-in affordances that were created by their designer. A hammer, for example, has a heavy metal end and a slimmer wooden end. Both are there to serve a specific purpose and were put there by a human intelligence. As a result, both have uses suggested by their shape and materials.

All human tools have such affordances, and our ability to notice them makes up the core of what it means for a tool to have a set of "perceived affordances." The notion of perceived affordances was made popular by Don Norman in *The Design of Everyday Things* (Norman, 2013)—a book focused on how design elements in everyday things signal their proper use. The flip side of perceived affordances is that when problems arise, they are generally a result of missing or misleading design elements.

This is because we often act on what perceived affordances suggest in unconscious ways. When I was a graduate student in Ann Arbor, Michigan (Go Blue!), for example, I visited a candy store whose door had two handles, one on the inside and one on the outside (so far so good). The issue with this particular door is that both handles were the same—they were both "pull" handles (as opposed to push plates common on doors found in some shops).

Normally when one sees a pull handle on a door, the intuition is to *pull* on the handle to open the door. Yet, when folks (including me) pulled on the handle facing the street, the door wouldn't open—it would close. This led to a steady stream of *crash* sounds as folks collided with a door they expected to open when they pulled on a handle—one whose *perceived affordance* was to be pulled. This caused enough issues over time that the store placed the following sign on the door, next to the door handle:

> This door doesn't open there way you think it does . . . unless you think it's a PUSH Door. Then you'd be right!

I'll never understand why they made a sign instead of replacing the outward facing door handle, as that would have been a better fix. Still, as the above example illustrates, perceived affordances in everyday objects matter because they suggest how we should interact with them. Pull handles on doors should be pulled to open the door, whereas push plates on doors should be pushed to open the door.

All door handles—indeed all designed objects—have perceived affordances because human designers build them into their designs. A given tool is usually deliberately designed in a manner that suggests its function. If you think carefully about the design of objects around you at any given time, it should become clear that many of the tools you use have such affordances.

This notion of a tool's design suggesting how it should be used is not confined to physical objects; the same can be said for digital objects. User experience (UX) designers do similar work (e.g., Pucillo & Cascini, 2014), which is why using a smartphone is (generally) a frictionless experience. Icons that launch apps mimic buttons. You "click on" or "press" a digital button expecting it to behave roughly how a physical button would. This haptic feedback has been shown to help with tasks such as wayfinding (Azenkot et al., 2011).

The core contribution of Norman's perceived affordances concept is that we can regularly interrogate the design elements of all human-made objects and tools to begin to make sense of how they might be used. In fact, I would argue that *all* human designs have similar signals to users so that the chances a tool is used correctly are maximized, and a tool is used incorrectly is minimized. The trick is examining what a tool can do.

This is also true of GenAI technologies. For this notion to be useful, we have to break away from seeing GenAI tools as fundamentally different; all GenAI applications are tools. They can be wonderful tools, but they are nonetheless tools. Consequently, when we consider GenAI and its potential impact on education, it is important not to misattribute *human* intelligence to GenAI where there is none. This includes recent calls to conceptualize our interaction with GenAI tools as a type of "hybrid" intelligence (Järvelä et al., 2025).

Such metaphors are naive and reinforce the idea that GenAI tools have proto-human intelligence and, as such, we should interact with them as "peers," "collaborators," "partners," or other human-like relationships. They are none of these things. GenAI tools, as instantiated through chat (or chat-like) interfaces, are merely *Synthetic Human Language Machines*. They create language data.

For a time, we were convinced that language data was uniquely human. It turns out it isn't. There were similar debates surrounding computation and the first calculators, and we've (rightly) moved on from those debates (Ellington, 2003). Falling into the trap of seeing GenAI as more than a tool is understandable, but doing so does more harm than good in the long run, and does a disservice to our students who look to us to make sense of how they should be engaging with these new technologies.

Instead, we should situate GenAI tools, applications, and so on, as strictly non-human technologies so that we nurture proper interactions that are not predicated on attributing a sense of humanity to technology that is *fundamentally* not human and not intelligent. Instead, GenAI applications are simply a subset of digital tools, and it is important for us to examine them as such.

Heidegger's Philosophy of Tools

Tools are everywhere. We make them, use them, break them, celebrate them, and criticize them. Tool use is so thoroughly embedded in what it means to be human, in fact, that anthropologists use tool use as evidence of human (or human-like) intelligence both in our ancestors (Gibson & Ingold, 1993), as well as other animal species like corvids (Jacobs & Osvath, 2023). It is no surprise, then, that as human beings our capabilities and identities are often intertwined with the tools we use. (Think of surnames that have their genesis in crafts associated with tool use, like "Carpenter," "Baker," "Smith," etc.)

Tools, and how we engage with them, are so important to our everyday lives that Martin Heidegger's ontology (Heidegger, 1962) explicitly explores humanity through an examination of tools. ("Ontology" is just a philosophical term for the study of "being.") In Heidegger's case, and in mine, the primary concern is to examine human phenomena through tool use.

In *Being and Time*, Martin Heidegger asserts that human beings can be best understood through a systematic study of how we engage with the world around us. Indeed, throughout the text of *Being and Time*, Heidegger does not refer to human beings as "humans" or "persons," and instead uses "*Dasein*," which can be roughly translated as "being there," "presence," or "existence."

Thus, to be human is to be engaged with the world one inhabits—to be a "Human *be*-ing." This position is not merely a description of what we do as humans (e.g., interact with our world) and instead focuses on the notion that to *be* human is to *engage* with the world. Being human, and engaging with the world, are inseparable. We cannot be one without the other.

Thus, if we are to study humanity, we must focus on how we interact with the world around us. It is beyond the scope of this book to dig too deeply into the philosophical implications and limitations of this claim, however. Instead, I take the above claim and use it as a useful framework for you to think about GenAI tools and the implications of their use.

Before that, however, it is useful to dig into how Heidegger builds his argument. In §15 of *Being and Time*, Heidegger states: "Taken strictly, there is no such thing as an equipment"(Heidegger, 1962, p. 97). "Equipment" for our purposes, is synonymous with "tool." This is a core point of the work—equipment only makes sense in relation to a specific context, one that is filled with other types of equipment. A keyboard, for example, is only fully functional so long as it is also surrounded by other things that enable its use (e.g., the computer and the user).

If I were to place a lonely keyboard at the bottom of the ocean it would not only be useless, it might begin to lose its meaning. Taken to its logical conclusion, a keyboard is, strictly speaking, no longer a keyboard without the corresponding objects that enable its core functionality. This notion is what Heidegger calls "a totality of equipment" (Heidegger, 1962, p. 97).

If we dig into this idea a little more, we see that Heidegger proposes that "[to] the Being of any equipment there always belongs a totality of equipment, in which it can be this equipment that it is" (p. 97). If Heidegger's words feel a little abstract, that's OK; the main takeaway is that tools ("equipment") lose meaning when they're outside of their context of use ("the totality"). This totality, then, represents a set of necessary contextual factors that give rise to a tool's core function. When any one piece is missing—or broken—the totality breaks down. Basically, if you take a tool away from the things that make it work, it is no longer useful. (Like the keyboard at the bottom of the ocean.)

Therefore, in a very literal sense, a tool must be connected to all other tools in the system to not only function but to exist in the fullest sense. Similarly, GenAI tools do not fully exist unless they are enacted in tandem with the data that drives their function, the interfaces we use to engage with them (computers), and within the contexts where they are useful.

It is, in fact, difficult to think of a GenAI tool that is fully divorced from the data and contexts that underpin its use. For example, a GenAI tool without the large corpus of words that drives its LLMs is simply a set of rules that cannot function. Similarly, all functions associated with GenAI lose meaning without *users*. The important practical and ethical considerations when it comes to GenAI tools, then, lie at the nexus of design, use, and context—the sociotechnical system I defined earlier.

Heidegger's core point is that tools—regardless of their use—are intertwined in a dependent system. This suggests that it is unlikely (or impossible) for a tool to exist in a vacuum. Heidegger takes this idea to its logical conclusion: the fact that all tools are intertwined forces us to conclude that without the appropriate referents, a given tool cannot be properly *perceived*.

This happens all the time. For example, you can browse Reddit's popular sub-reddit "what is this thing" (Reddit, n.d.) and read posts from users that include images of tools that confuse them. Such tools have no functional existence until their use is collectively discovered by other users. When I give talks I often use an image of an "apple butter paddle" to reinforce this point, as it is a niche tool that is hard to parse without context. I make it a habit to pull images from the *r/whatisthisthing* because they are perfect examples of tools out-of-context, tools that cannot function because their intended uses are not easily understood.

Here's where it gets complicated. The above argument does not suggest that we can simply reduce tools to a set of functions or parts that operate independently from their whole. Heidegger asserts that in perceiving a room we do not see space that is between four walls, a floor, and a ceiling; we simply see a room, or "[an] equipment for residing" (98). (You can blame the awkward phrasing on the German to English translation.)

Therefore, although it may be useful to distinguish between features of tools to examine their purpose, doing so creates artificial distinctions relative to their use. Tools are always a part of a "web" of interrelated tools and contexts. So, just as a painting cannot be understood by examining an individual brush stroke in isolation, one cannot understand tools by isolating them from other tools. The sociotechnical system is thus not merely a three-dimensional interaction of one tool, one person, and one context. It is a complex web of many tools, many users, and many contexts; all of which overlap in ways that can be difficult to tease apart.

Yet, we can still interrogate tools. Tools can show their *ontological characteristics*, that is, how they behave out in the world, or as Heidegger would put it: “Equipment can genuinely show itself only in the dealings cut to its own measure” (98). Hence my keyboard only shows itself to be a keyboard when I am typing, like now.

That is why many times as adults we show children (and other adults) what different tools are used for via demonstration. If we simply told someone: “a keyboard is used for typing,” they would then want to know what typing was. Yet, if instead we take the time to show the same individual the process of typing, then they would likely begin to understand the nature of what it was to “be” a keyboard, that is, a tool used to convert keystrokes into letters on a screen.

This is not to say that we cannot understand the *ontological character* of tools by being told what they do, however. Heidegger simply states that we cannot fully understand tools unless we see them doing what they are meant to do (hammer hammering, knife cutting, keyboard typing, etc.). It is also important to note that when we use tools, the web of “connected-ness” that they are a part of is not visible to us. Put concretely, I do not think about my keyboard in relation to the monitor or the computer. I simply type and for the most part ignore everything else.

Ready-to-Hand vs. Present-at-Hand

Phew. You did it. You got through some Heidegger. At this point you might be wondering why I bothered to bring Heidegger into a book about GenAI in education. Thinking about *ontology* through the lens of a dead German philosopher may feel tiresome, but it is nonetheless a powerful—and useful—exercise. We don’t often take the time to think about tools in the persnickety ways Heidegger did, but once we do we find that we can begin to make sense of many different tools in our everyday lives, including GenAI.

To recap, tools have uses, and those uses can be understood as their *being*. We can further understand more about ourselves by examining our relationship to tools. To do so we need only pose a few questions such as: How do we use tools? How do we *not* use tools? How do we learn to use tools and teach others to use them? Such questions enable us to better understand both the tools themselves and our relationship to them.

Heidegger's ontology may feel foreign, but enacted parts of it drive the points I am making in this book. For example, we should disabuse ourselves of the notion that GenAI is so special that we need to avoid thinking about it as a tool. It is not special, it is merely novel. GenAI is a tool, and we should understand it as such. By doing so, moreover, we can understand ourselves, our goals, and GenAI's relationship to education.

Thus, "tool-use" helps us better understand how GenAI's design affordances play a key role in educational technologies. A GenAI application, for example, can automate core components of the teaching process. Teachers can generate lesson plans, assignments, and other relevant artifacts necessary for students to master content. Importantly, however, using GenAI to do those things cedes some creative control to a set of algorithms that have, in turn, their own set of assumptions baked in.

Those "algorithmic assumptions" are inseparable from the assumptions held by developers of GenAI technologies, and the underlying data that power LLMs. Such assumptions can define what it means to be learner or instructor. GenAI, then, can be interpreted as the invisible arms of instruction that both contain and execute core assumptions and biases. It would be naive to assume that such data—and associated algorithms—are true (unbiased) representations of the world. Sometimes, in fact, such representations are problematic and cause harm. This is a point that Safiya Noble (2018) makes in *Algorithms of Oppression*.

There are two additional Heideggerian concepts that will be useful to us as we navigate GenAI: "ready-to-hand" and "present-at-hand." Both relate to how we interact with everyday tools and technologies. They are useful concepts because they enable me to illustrate how technology—in this case GenAI—can be seamlessly integrated into our activities or become perplexing objects of focus.

What does Heidegger mean, however, when he discusses "ready-to-hand" and "present-at-hand?" Before you ask, yes, the hyphens are necessary thanks to the German words they're derived from: *Vorhandenheit* and *Zuhandenheit*, which are—I'm told—a fun play on words.

"Ready-to-hand" tools are tools that you use so well that you forget that you're even using them. Experienced drivers, for example, do not actively think of driving, they just *drive* and can attend to distractions better than novice drivers (Kass et al., 2007). Similarly, elite athletes treat the tools of their sport (e.g., baseballs, basketballs, bats, etc.) as *extensions* of who they are. Musicians do the same.

In each of these examples, tools become unnoticed the moment they are mastered. Not only do they become unnoticed—they are in many ways extensions of their users. “Ready-to-hand” tools are used by everyone, every single day. Think of a tool that you use for your profession, your hobby, or your day-to-day life. If you’ve mastered it to the point where it becomes unnoticed during its use, then it is “ready-to-hand.”

“Present-at-hand” tools are the opposite. They are tools that are new, malfunctioning, broken, or otherwise used in a way that makes them salient. Think of using a broken hammer or using a laptop with aggressive malware. Both are examples of tools that are in a “present-at-hand” state; their salience makes them ineffective. Tools that are “present-at-hand,” however, are not always broken. They can simply be *new*.

Think of a sixteen-year-old learning how to drive a car. To them, the car is salient—it is “present-at-hand.” The same can be said for anyone learning how to play a new instrument or using an unfamiliar tool whose function is not obvious. Thus, whether or not a tool is “present-at-hand” or “ready-to-hand” is a function of the tool itself *and* its user.

To the sixteen-year-old teenager learning to drive, a car is an intimidating machine. They, as a novice driver, will be unable to simply drive, as they must attend to the steering wheel, the pedals, the shifter, the mirrors, and countless other aspects of the car. This inhibits their ability to drive, at least until they’ve “mastered the basics.” To a parent teaching their child to drive, the same car is “ready-to-hand.” The parent can simply hop in the car and drive without a second thought.

If it is helpful, you can think of the distinction between “present-at-hand” and “ready-to-hand” through the lens of *use*. Some tools are ready to use, others are not ready to use. Understanding *why* some tools are ready to be used, and why others aren’t, is at the core of understanding the distinction between “ready-to-hand” and “present-at-hand.”

Synthesizing Norman and Heidegger

Though they wrote decades apart from each other, I see Norman’s (2013) framework for understanding the design affordances of objects and Heidegger’s ontology of equipment as complementary. Heidegger focused on thought experiments to examine the "being" of tools and our relationship to them. Norman explored the world around us and understood that tools suggest how they should be used through a set of perceptible design affordances. Both approaches have implications for how we might better understand GenAI's impacts on education.

But first, let's return to a common physical tool: the hammer. Upon picking up a hammer you might notice that it is clearly a hand tool, and that one end is heavy and metallic. While this may not immediately suggest that the heavy end of a hammer should connect with a nail, it does suggest that it can be swung to connect with another object. This is the central thesis of Norman's design affordances. When tools are closely examined, their potential purposes can reveal themselves to us. Designed objects we encounter in our daily life thus suggest to us affordances that we either implicitly or explicitly attend to as we use them.

Often, these design affordances are obvious. A lighter claw hammer will have distinct affordances when compared to its heavier cousin, the sledge hammer. Other times the affordances are more nuanced and informed by professional standards; a drywall hammer will have a different use than a claw hammer, for example.

Now let's layer on Heidegger. When the design of the hammer disagrees with its function, an object that should be "ready-to-hand" shifts into being "present-at-hand." Try using a sledgehammer to drive a nail into the wall to hang a frame, and you'll understand what I mean. Similarly, I challenge you to drive a nail with a hammer that has a broken shaft tapped together with one loop of flimsy painter's tape. Both attempts will end in tragedy for your wall (or your hand).

This is Heidegger's contribution to our discussion. Tools, be they digital or analog, can—and should be—understood as operating in one of two states: "ready-to-hand" or "present-at-hand." The former state is characterized by seamlessly using a tool effectively. When one has mastered the use of a tool—and the tool itself is functional—it recedes from notice when it is being used to accomplish a specific task.

On the other hand, when tools are noticed and unusable they are "present-at-hand." A broken hammer, for example, is noticeable because it is unusable, yet it is still identifiable as a tool. "Present-at-hand" does not only apply to broken tools. An *unfamiliar* tool is just as unusable as a broken one because its core function is not fully understood. You might not know what a "dead blow" hammer is for, for example. (Look it up, they're neat!)

Back to GenAI. Currently, we are in the midst of understanding what GenAI is *for*. This requires us to attend to the design affordances of a given GenAI tool so that we can use it. A chatbot, for example, invites us to "chat." It's even in the name of OpenAI's flagship product: *Chat*GPT. Yet, not all GenAI tool uses are obvious. Thus, our use of any GenAI tool can oscillate between being "present-at-hand" and "ready-to-hand."

Consequently, the current state of GenAI in education feels chaotic. GenAI affordances are developing, as are its primary use-cases. This creates a dissonance that must be resolved in order for GenAI tools to become useful instruments of pedagogical practice and/or tools that help students study and learn.

Algorithms

GenAI tools are obviously digital and not physical. This should not concern us, however, as the distinction between physical tools and digital tools is not new to GenAI. Before the explosion of GenAI tools, the discourse was squarely on understanding the consequences of "black box" algorithms on learning, including unpacking their affordances and limitations. What are algorithms, however?

No matter when they are designed and by whom, algorithms have a set of design affordances that either suggest or dictate how they can be used. Before we can discuss such affordances, however, it is important to establish a common definition for what an algorithm is, and what it does. I use Donald E. Knuth's (1997) definition to guide this discussion.

Knuth defines algorithms as "a finite set of rules that gives a sequence of operations for solving a specific type of problem." This definition is comprised of four components. First, algorithms are "finite," so they have clear boundaries. This means that they have limitations that both users and their designers need to contend with. Second, algorithms are a "set of rules" that dictate their function. Using Norman's (2013) language, we can parse rules contained within algorithms as their design affordances.

Third, an algorithm's set of affordances (rules) leads to a "sequence of operations." Put plainly, once an algorithm is executed "things happen," much like when the first domino in a chain is knocked over. Using our new Heideggerian language, the set of operations can be understood as the tool "in use." Finally, algorithms act on "specific" problems, which can be understood as a set of tasks that an algorithm is well-suited to act on—just like a hammer is well-suited to hammer a nail into a wooden board.

Thus, algorithms are simply tools, and as tools they are instantiations of a designer's perspective. When designed well, algorithms are innovative and help make tasks more efficient. When designed poorly, however, algorithms express problematic biases and limited understanding of the context they purport to act on. This can perpetuate—or accelerate—poor outcomes. For algorithms to be designed ethically within GenAI, it becomes imperative to foreground the perspectives that inform their design. In so doing, we can detect when GenAI tools have the potential to go awry in educational settings.

Before GenAI, this process was well underway. Academic studies, for example, have focused on algorithms embedded within educational technologies. The goal of such studies focused on documenting, preventing, and/or mitigating the negative impact of uninterrogated algorithms. This has been shown to be particularly important for underserved student populations (e.g., racial/ethnic minorities and women), as well as less studied groups (e.g., linguistic minorities, military connected status) (Baker & Hawn, 2021).

This imperative to slow down and examine algorithms was necessary, in part, because the field of Edtech has moved toward personalizing the experience of students at all levels (e.g., Portugal et al., 2018; Brooks et al., 2011; Fancsali, 2011; Teplovs, 2011). This includes predicting which students might need extra support (e.g., Atkisson & Wiley, 2011; Suthers & Rosen, 2011), and communicating those insights via user-facing dashboards (Aguilar, 2022; Aguilar et al., 2021; Verbert et al., 2013; Park et al., 2015; Sedrakyan et al., 2020).

Algorithms played—and continue to play—a large and necessary part in EdTech innovation. Without them, personalization at-scale and "at-speed" would not be possible. GenAI technologies are simply extensions of this work. Still, the proliferation of algorithm-driven educational technologies created an imperative to carefully examine them to better understand their affordances and shortcomings (i.e., Norman), as well as how they behaved out in the world (Heidegger). Work in this area showed that despite the nearing ubiquity of personalized learning experiences for students, the field still has an identifiable blind spot when it comes to issues of diversity and equity (e.g., Baker & Hawn, 2021; Kordzadeh & Ghasemaghaei, 2022; Baek & Aguilar, 2022; Williamson & Kizilcec 2021).

Algorithms are a good use-case to examine under our framework, because they may seem, on the face of it, to be abstractions that cannot be reduced to any meaningful physical characteristics. Rather than consider them to be mere abstractions, however, I suggest that algorithms can be best understood as both static and dynamic instantiations of human decisions. They are static because they operate as adjudicators governed by a set of rules created by their designers. They are dynamic because they can be changed based on changing circumstances—either in near-real time or after a period of audit where it is determined that they are operating in a manner that is suboptimal.

All of this is also true of GenAI technologies that are simply governed by a different set of algorithms driven by large language foundation models. While we cannot quickly and easily examine the embedded affordances of GenAI tools within educational technologies, it is still important to establish a framework for how one might go about doing so. GenAI tools vis-à-vis their use within a given context provide an opportunity to do so. Thus, it is important to examine their deployment in different educational settings.

Returning to the Synthetic Human Language Machine

When it comes to GenAI in educational settings, we must remember that there is a human who makes key decisions about how a given GenAI application will function. It was an entirely human decision, for example, for ChatGPT to signal that it is "thinking," when it is, in fact, merely taking the time to process data and generate output. Gone are the days of rainbow spinners, it seems.

Further, designers who create and deploy GenAI educational technologies make explicit (or implicit) claims about learning itself. The goal when examining the use-cases of GenAI, then, is to interrogate those claims and uncover potential unintended consequences. This will allow us to wrestle with the practical and ethical implications of how GenAI is used in education.

Now that Norman (2013) and Heidegger have given us a working vocabulary when interrogating the use of a tool, we can apply those terms to GenAI. We can reframe GenAI applications not as "intelligences" that we have to work with as pseudo-peers, but instead as tools. As machines that we command and whose output we are responsible for.

To do this effectively, I believe that we need to change our language, to see GenAI not as an intelligence, but instead as a *Synthetic Human Artifact Machine*. As I've discussed elsewhere, this is not merely a rhetorical move on my part. It is an important mental framework that enables us to think of the affordances of GenAI as well as its limitations. It enables us to use the tool, while putting mitigations in place to ensure that the tool does not cause harm. This also requires us to move away from discourse that we might have already become comfortable with. One that posits that GenAI technologies are human-like.

You do not, for example, "build a relationship," with a hammer. Similarly, it is ludicrous to "build a relationship" with GenAI tools. Instead, you give GenAI data that it can use to further shape (i.e., bias) the output it generates. This is not the same as a relationship, at least not one we should aspire to build, as it is the same sort of relationship narcissists have with individuals whom they harm (e.g., Muris et al., 2017). Indeed, recent work suggests that the sycophancy that is endemic to GenAI inflates people's self-evaluations and can pull them toward echo chambers; so much so that "critical" GenAI interactions are seen as biased, while sycophantic ones are seen as neutral (Rathje et al., 2025). While such use may increase engagement, it is death to critical thinking.

Instead, the relationship with GenAI is purely transactional. How then, might we think of the transaction in education? If OpenAI's ChatGPT were more honest, then it would pose its first question as "what sort of synthetic knowledge would you like to generate today?" Perhaps not a catchy slogan, but an honest one that speaks to the affordance of the technology. What synthetic language might an educator need? At the K12 level, perhaps altering the reading level of a text so that all students could access it. Students, moreover, might need to generate synthetic language that could help with ideation, or ask GenAI to create synthetic language that gave them feedback on some of their own writing.

By now my use of "synthetic" might read as tortured, but that is done deliberately. Synthetic language generated by a machine suggests the existence of authentic language generated by a human. Moreover, we have a tendency to be wary of the synthetic, or at least treat it as different, as we need to determine its use and evaluate its *usefulness*.

I emphasize that synthetic things aren't bad! They are just different. Synthetic pigments in paints, for example, are used because they are both less expensive to manufacture and because some non-synthetic pigments (e.g., Cadmium Red) contain heavy metals that can be hazardous if the right precautions aren't taken. To use synthetic versus natural pigments is a choice informed by the context of use.

Artists might be fine with the risks associated with using Cadmium Red because they value its vibrancy and know how to handle the paint in a way that minimizes harm. They might also be willing to spend the money to buy it, as it is very expensive compared to alternatives. Similarly, a new art student might not work with Cadmium Red because they do not want to deal with the hazards and they do not have the money to buy it.

How might educators treat synthetic human language? It is, for one, much less effortful and easily generated. At least that is the user's perception, as there are many environmental considerations that are often glossed over. Still, what are we to do with synthetic language? We can, for instance, improve it by editing and adding authentic human language. We can treat it as a consumable that has little inherent value because it was not derived from human cognitive effort.

The Affordances of GenAI in Education

The technologies we use and integrate into our everyday lives reflect our values—of how we think work ought to be performed. Thus, when choosing tools, we must understand them and be mindful that their use does not undermine our core ethical principles. Norman and Heidegger have given us ways to better understand tool design and tool use. When examining GenAI, a clear affordance emerges—pattern recognition and generation. Human beings are great at recognizing patterns, and much of that power comes from our growing up in communities that enable us to be a part of cultures with shared understandings (Hausfather, 1996).

Take, for example, the following list of ingredients: tomatoes, basil, garlic, fresh pasta (pick your favorite), and ground beef. Now think for a moment, what can you make with this list of ingredients? I cannot read your mind, but I suspect you may have landed on something like ground beef spaghetti, or another similar pasta dish. There are a finite number of things you can make with the above ingredients, and what you can make is based on two things: (1) your understanding of how those ingredients work and taste, and (2) your knowledge of how those ingredients can be combined.

This is one of the key affordances of GenAI technologies—the ability to take one set of patterns (ingredients) and yield a different set of patterns (dishes). In education, this affordance can be applied to domain-specific tasks, such as having students get feedback on their writing or providing spaces for ideation.

All the while, however, it is important to realize that we are not communicating with an intelligence. Instead, are using a Synthetic Human Artifact Machine, and should thus be mindful of what we input into those machines. For example, we should avoid submitting sensitive information. We should also question the quality of the synthetic content. It is our responsibility to detect erroneous information ("hallucinations").

This enables us to better understand GenAI technologies as akin to a kitchen appliance that ingests *millions* of recipes and downloads *millions* of hours of cooking shows. After all, it's a mere matter of statistics to determine what dishes are more likely to be prepared given a list of ingredients. This is why I introduced the terms "Synthetic Human Language Machine" and "Synthetic Human Artifact Machine" in the first place. Given inputs, you gain outputs. The outputs, moreover, are based on what the inputs are. It is a closed system of statistical inference—one that mimics intelligence because the ingredients are language (or other human artifacts), but one that cannot *reason* in the same way we can.

Given that using GenAI can be reduced to using *any* tool, it is important to note that educators are under no special obligation to accept the claims of GenAI tool developers. They have just cause to question both developers' intentions while also interrogating GenAI tool designs. Interrogating the designs of any given GenAI tool will enable educators to better understand its potential affordances.

Once educators have grasped the key affordances, they can begin to see what mastery over the tools yields (ready-to-hand), as well as what hurdles need to be overcome to move from present-at-hand use to ready-to-hand use. This tripartite approach will enable educators to move beyond the anxieties of the AI-alarmists, while also avoiding the hollow promises of the AI-zealots.

At every turn in this process it is equally important to ensure that all parties within the sociotechnical system are aware of what GenAI tools can do, and what they can't. Tools do not work well unless they operate in contexts that enable their use. Keeping this at the forefront of how we use GenAI tools will enable us to better understand the implications of adopting GenAI technologies into educational settings. This will enable optimism based on pragmatism and allow us to understand the limitations of GenAI tools to ensure that they enhance, rather than undermine, the educational process.

5

Avoiding Imaginary Enemies

Chapter Outline

Introduction

Whenever new technologies emerge, there is a metaphorical gold rush, and at least two sets of opportunists. There are opportunists selling the new technology and their "expertise" on how it can be best used. There are also opportunists selling the status quo, coupled with lectures or other services to inoculate you against the dangers of the new technology. Both perspectives are myopic and self-interested. Neither will help you *understand* the new technology. I've characterized both sides as either AI-zealots, or AI-alarmists.

I often find that the ideas of AI-alarmists can be the most insidious, because they seemingly come from a place of "doing good." Unfortunately, AI-alarmist perspectives often fall into the trope of *tilting at windmills*, a concept that first appeared in Don Quixote, where the protagonist (Quixote) wished to attack the "giants" he perceived:

> ". . . for you can see over there, good friend Sancho Panza, a place where stand thirty or more monstrous giants with whom I intend to fight a battle and whose lives I intend to take . . . [f]or this is a just war, and it is a great service to God to wipe such a wicked breed from the face of the earth."
>
> "What giants?" said Sancho Panza.
>
> "Those giants that you can see over there," replied his master, "with long arms: there are giants with arms almost six miles long."
>
> "Look you here," Sancho retorted, "those over there aren't giants, they're windmills, and what look to you like arms are sails. . . ." (Cervantes, 2016/1605)

For Don Quixote, tilting at windmills was literal; mounted knights of his day would tilt down their lances as they charged toward their enemies. In contemporary times, tilting at windmills is metaphorical, though no less irrational.

AI-alarmists cherry-pick problematic use-cases of GenAI, like academic dishonesty (Cotton et al., 2024), or cognitive laziness (Fan et al., 2025). They then argue that such use-cases are reason enough to avoid the technology altogether (e.g., Fenton, 2024). They do so despite mixed evidence on students' actual cheating behaviors (e.g., Macias & Aguilar, 2026; Huang et al., 2025). AI-alarmists are the Don Quixotes of our day. They misperceive GenAI tools as monstrous giants, either through ignorance or cynicism. Moreover, they signal that *they* are best positioned to defeat the "monster" of GenAI.

When we fall prey to the negative speculation proffered by AI-alarmists, we become Don Quixote ourselves and battle imaginary enemies we erroneously perceive as threats. This isn't to say that there are no negative use-cases of GenAI, there are and they should be studied, however there is a difference between seeing what's real (windmills) versus imagining harms (giants).

In this chapter I describe four such imagined enemies: unchecked negative bias; agentic AI; the erosion of critical thinking; and the loss of academic integrity among students. Proponents of these negative aspects of GenAI do not account for the sociotechnical system where GenAI technologies operate (Chapter 3), or the design affordances of GenAI technologies (Chapter 4). In so doing, they create imagined enemies to battle. This instructive parallel—between Quixote's "giants" and today's hyperbolic warnings about AI—serves as a warning to get us to refocus on what is important when discussing the possibilities afforded by GenAI in education.

Rethinking "Bias"

The first dimension of GenAI that people treat as a monster is "bias." This may seem surprising to some, but there is a tendency to erroneously couple bias in GenAI with *negative* imagery that evokes feelings of injustice. Further, bias is often conceptualized as necessarily leading to negative—or differing—experiences based on factors that are outside of the user's control (e.g., Warikoo et al., 2016; Druckman et al., 2021).

These presuppositions with respect to bias are understandable, as we often think of bias by reflecting on its effects on our institutions and rightly recalling injustices or problematic patterns. In education, we might, for example, consider the efforts put in place to mitigate long-standing disparities (e.g., Baker & Knight, 2025).

We might also consider bias that is associated with college admissions, such as giving legacy candidates a leg up in admissions decisions (Castilla & Poskanzer, 2022). There is also gender bias that appears on student evaluations, where women receive lower ratings for no other (statistical) reason than being women (Heffernan, 2022). Given this context, our initial reactions are justifiably focused on "eliminating" bias or developing mitigations that lessen its effects (e.g., Woo et al., 2023).

There is also bias in our professional settings. There has been work that has shown qualified candidates getting passed over for job interviews because of their ethnic sounding names, despite having the same exact credentials as candidates with western names (Bertrand & Mullainathan, 2004). On an individual level, many of us may also be on guard, wondering if the actions of others are somehow driven by perceptions tied to some aspect of our identity. This can create—or exasperate—feelings of imposter syndrome or stereotype threat (Sonnak & Towell, 2001; Steele & Aronson, 1995).

Bias is insidious and appears everywhere. When we shift our attention to bias and *technology*, many examples come to mind, such as bias found in big data algorithms that drive search results (O'Neil, 2017). We might also recall seminal work that found bias in data sets that train the machine learning algorithms in many everyday technologies, creating imagery based on stereotypes rather than reality (Noble, 2018).

All of the above examples have a similar defining characteristic: bias leads to negative outcomes because biased systems attend to certain dimensions over others. These differences are not trivial, as they result in negative lived experiences and outcomes for those affected. Those on the losing side of bias often feel alienated (Brown et al., 2003), while others' find that their capabilities are overestimated, granting them unearned advantages (Tobisch & Dresel, 2017). Given this, there are many calls to "eliminate" bias and move toward "objectivity." It is unsurprising that bias has become an important topic of study, as well as solutions to bias. It is further understandable that notions of bias have become an area of focus for those who are concerned about the negative impact of GenAI on education.

Why, then, do I suggest that "bias" is a windmill posing as a monster in the current discourse? What *is* bias, and how can we better understand it so that we can meaningfully engage with each other during discussions of bias in GenAI systems? I'll begin by being blunt: I do not find overly negative definitions of bias useful in discussions about GenAI because they tend to evoke feelings of both righteousness and defensiveness.

The study and rectifying of bias has become a cottage industry in education—one that requires righteous defenders fighting against (presumably evil) antagonists. I do not find that discourse useful. Instead, I find that such efforts tend to lead to uninteresting discussions with regard to GenAI. The "windmill," then, is characterized by an oversimplification of bias followed by a myopic focus on supposed "solutions."

I offer a fuller definition of bias—one that is not inherently negative and one that suggests courses of action based on desired (or desirable) outcomes. I'll start with the obvious: bias is an unavoidable part of the human condition and is synonymous with perspective. As such, it is neither uniformly harmful nor uniformly positive. Instead, it is a predictable part of any system reflecting human input.

This *includes* the data we collect (all of it) as well as the algorithms derived from human decisions. It also includes *us*; there is no such thing as an "objective" human being because when we make decisions we do so using schema and knowledge that we've gained during our lifetimes. Every human being thus *knows* different things, though there is overlap based on upbringing, training, and so on. Further, we have not been neutral parties in the knowledge we develop or disseminate. We make choices about which topics warrant study, which areas deserve our inquisitive gaze, and whom we share our insights with.

Thus, humans are *necessarily* biased. This idea is somewhat captured by the popular notion of "positionally" in education research (Bourke, 2014), though I have not found positionality statements particularly useful, as they seem to be predicated on the notion that naming bias eliminates it or serves as a mitigator. It does neither. The only way to gain a fuller understanding of a system is to include *more* perspectives—at all levels. When considering GenAI, this means more data from more people and evaluated by a diversity of expertise.

I imagine that at this point my above claims have caused a non-trivial number of readers to bristle—but hear me out. When I teach statistical methods, I often have to push students to unlearn the common definition of bias (something negative to be eliminated) toward the more technical definition. This definition can be used just as effectively to make similar points.

If we start from the premise that all human actions and decisions are biased (yes, *all* of them), we can begin to examine *how* they are biased and determine if the bias is warranted and/or leads to desirable outcomes. Once we do that, we can shift our perceptions to the real concern: reducing bias that perpetuates harmful stereotypes, finding and eliminating blind spots in our data, and moving toward data systems that capture key dimensions of the populations we wish to serve.

This is best accomplished through seeing bias as a tool that has inherent affordances and limitations. Thus, a technical definition of bias enables us to take further actions. To investigate, interrogate, and shape bias, rather than treating it as a static entity that can be excised like one would remove a cancer from a body.

Bias in GenAI

Given the above argument, there are numerous ways that bias can hobble GenAI-driven educational technologies. As I've outlined elsewhere, GenAI technologies are, at their heart, *Synthetic Human Artifact Machines* (SHAMs). If we start with bias as our first premise, and the notion that outputs from GenAI are synthetic as our second, we can begin to interrogate the ingredients that lead to GenAI outputs.

Here are some sample questions that one could ask in this vein:

- *How* are GenAI tools biased, and what data drives the bias? (As opposed to wondering "if" they're biased.)
- What *data* has been used to train (i.e., bias) the GenAI tool?

- Can a GenAI tool be further personalized (biased) to better attend to the unique features of the potential user group (e.g., students vs. teachers)
- How are "guardrails" defined, and what sorts of bias are addressed with them?

The above questions are not meant to be exhaustive. Instead, they are examples that are intended to give you a way to think of bias as something you can understand at a technical level. These questions can help you interrogate the usefulness of GenAI tools. This shift in how you think of bias will enable more productive outcomes, as bias becomes a tool that you can closely examine.

When speaking to vendors, administrators from educational institutions would do well to pose questions similar to those above. If bias feels incorrect, one can use "personalized" with similar effectiveness. The goal is to understand the bias and use it. For their part, vendors would do well to be explicit about the bias in their GenAI systems by being clear about the data that was used to train them. This enables us to move on from seeing bias as a windmill to charge and defeat. Bias is complex, and its complexity should not be reduced to a monster we charge in hopes of destroying it.

Attributing Human Agency to GenAI

GenAI applications are exciting, and for good reason—they create artifacts that we once thought were uniquely human (e.g., coherent prose and visual art). The trouble with this innovation is that there is a growing discourse that mistakenly ascribes human-like agency to GenAI technologies. Most of the time this happens when we mistakenly call GenAI technologies "intelligent." This is a core misunderstanding that has been perpetuated by companies like OpenAI, where Sam Altman, its CEO, says things like:

> My kids will never be smarter than AI . . . [t]hey will grow up vastly more capable than we grew up and able to do things that we just, we cannot imagine. And they'll be really good at using AI. (Freedman, 2025)

The second half of this sentence is true on its face. As technology progresses, those who use it become more capable *of using that technology*. Yet, this does not necessarily mean that those born into new technologies are any smarter than those who were not born into them. This point should be obvious, but often gets lost in the push to make GenAI technologies seem more than they are.

Take the ongoing joke that Millennials (born between 1981 and 1996) are members of the only generation to have mastered using a desktop computer effectively. Baby boomers (1946–64) and Gen X (1965–80) were born too early. Gen Z (1997–2012) and Gen Alpha (2013–24) were born too late. The latter generations have been shown to demonstrate more comfort using smartphones than desktop or laptop computers, for example (McGraw-Hill Education, 2015; Denoyelles et al., 2023).

There is no mystery here—one acclimates to the technologies that exist in the world one was born into. That is perfectly fine and perfectly human. Generational differences in comfort with technology are not indicators of intelligence. To think otherwise would be to tacitly endorse the idea that those who grew up with electricity are smarter than those who grew up without it. Yet, flipping a light switch is simply a different task compared to lighting a candle. We acclimate to the technologies that surround us as we develop. This process is distinct from intelligence.

Why, then, would Altman claim that his kids "will never be smarter than AI"? I'll bracket, for a second, my intuition that suspects Altman to be more of a salesman than an innovator. (That is, after all, the goal of the CEO—to ensure that their company grows and "creates value.") If I instead take the statement at face value, then I am forced to conclude that Altman simply has an impoverished view of human intelligence. Human intelligence is not merely the ability to recall facts when a question is posed. Even if we stay squarely within declarative knowledge, knowing *which* question to ask is *at least* as important as knowing the answer.

This is what separates, for example, Master's students from PhD students, the former are tasked with mastering the knowledge that exists, while the latter are tasked with generating new knowledge. PhD students are required to both know what is and propose what could be—that is the entire purpose of the dissertation. It is an inherently creative process.

Will Altman's children "know" more than GenAI? Probably, as GenAI doesn't actually "know" anything, it merely reproduces what *we* know in a manner that is fast and friendly. Or, if we define knowing as simply harboring knowledge, then the answer might be "no," but this is different than what *intelligence* is. To state otherwise is to reduce human beings to input/output machines without acknowledging rich inner worlds that matter just as much (or more) than what we are able to produce.

Altman's stance has obvious metaphysical considerations, but my criticism of it is pragmatic. If we see new GenAI technologies as *intelligent* and misattribute agency to them (i.e., autonomous human-like intelligences capable of true independent actions), then we will cease to see such technologies as tools to be leveraged for improving learning outcomes. Moreover, if we communicate those perspectives to students, then we create the potential for students to further misattribute humanness to mere tools.

Current generation GenAI tools are useful as Synthetic Human Artifact Machines, as not all human artifacts need to be truly creative endeavors. Many of the things we produce are perfectly fine as commodities. While this newfound capability to generate language is nice, it is akin to the keyboard I am typing on generating letters, rather than writing everything by hand. Thus, while GenAI tools may appear intelligent, they are, in fact, advanced tools that can accelerate tasks by using vast amounts of data. They are not intelligent agents that act with independent cognition.

A part of being human is seeing patterns and structure in a world that feels random. Whether we discover patterns and structures (the sciences) or create them (the arts and humanities), authentic human intelligence is more than the mere recall of what came before. It urges us to push forward. GenAI, for all its capabilities, is stuck in time. If I were to tell you that all you needed to know was held in a corpus of human language that was mainly in English and represented at best 100 years of written language, you would rightly consider me daft and reductive in the worst kind of way.

Academic Integrity and Authentic Learning

Perhaps one of the most persistent challenges with GenAI is that one of its key affordances makes it easy to generate academic work that is well-written. This issue is compounded by the fact that writing assignments are often structured in a way that are essentially prompts. In fact, when I was a middle school teacher I would literally write "writing *prompt*" at the top of a writing assignment I gave to my students. This can create an environment where academic dishonesty is effortless (McMurtrie, 2024; Madden et al., 2024).

It used to be that plagiarism, though problematic, forced students to engage with writing that they then passed off as their own. They would, presumably, read it and determine that it was valuable enough to masquerade as their own thoughts. With GenAI tools, a student can copy a prompt from a writing assignment, paste it into their GenAI chatbot of choice, and then turn in the generated synthetic text as though they were the ones who wrote it. This eliminates *all* engagement with authentic human writing, to the point where some students accidentally turn in the prompts along with the generated writing.

This low-level effort is easy to catch. Yet, more ambitious cheaters might choose to modify the text slightly, putting in some minimal effort, but less than is required to master content. This creates an unresolvable cat-and-mouse game, where students pretend that generated synthetic text is their own work, while educators read it knowing that it isn't, but without the ability to prove as much unless a student confesses.

It is clear that academic dishonesty is a real issue—why then do I discuss it in a chapter devoted to "avoiding imaginary enemies"? I'll start with the obvious: I agree that academic dishonesty via GenAI tools is a problem that needs to be addressed. What I disagree with, however, is the scope of the problem and common solutions to it.

This is why the next "imagined giant" is the notion that academic dishonesty is common among students. While some concern is valid, the threat of students constantly using GenAI to cheat is overblown. Cheating will always bypass the authentic learning process and make it difficult for teachers to assess students' actual understanding of content. Yet, cheating with GenAI requires superficial assignments, or low-level engagement of student work from educators.

In fact, there have been calls for decades to make assessment of student knowledge less superficial. This includes using both summative (e.g., final exams) and formative (e.g., short quizzes) assessments in classrooms (Glazer, 2014). The former serve as indicators of mastered content, while the latter enable educators to reevaluate their pedagogy and/or provide students with additional opportunities to master content.

Despite this, there have been many calls to "ban" the use of GenAI. Yet, if educators "ban" the use of GenAI, then what they are effectively doing is ignoring its use while also removing themselves as stewards of their classrooms. Doing so ignores the responsibility to respond to the world their students will engage with once they complete their formal education.

Bans do not work because they come with weak mechanisms of enforcement. "AI" detectors, for example, are not up to the task of truly detecting generated work (Mathewson, 2025). Such tools can cause educators to misattribute GenAI text to students, even if students wrote the work themselves. False positives are not mere inconveniences—they undermine students' motivation to continue to engage with work (Mathewson, 2023).

False positives also do not occur randomly. Instead, they mirror what we already know about bias in education. Students who are linguistic minorities, for example, will be simultaneously more susceptible to false positives, while also having fewer resources to combat erroneous accusations. This group includes students whose first language is not English (or the dominant language of the educational space), as they are more likely to use more rigid forms of writing as they begin to master a language that is not native to them.

This has the potential to demotivate students, undermine their confidence in their educational institutions, and also decrease the number of authentic learning opportunities. This can lead to a needlessly combative relationship between student and instructor, one where both suspect each other of wrongdoing (i.e., using AI to complete work and using AI to grade and make accusations of cheating). Such environments lacking in trust are the death of learning, as they tax cognitive resources, and also taint the incentive structure for instructor and student alike.

It is an unwinnable arms race. Students will learn how to game the system, rather than learn from it, and instructors will either give up entirely or double-down on reintroducing outdated instructional practices (e.g., Fenton, 2024). Educators may also spend more money on tools that are designed to catch students red-handed, rather than tools that help students engage with emerging GenAI technologies.

It is relatively easy to imagine what the internal dialogue of educators and students would sound like in this world of mistrust:

Educator: Why would I spend so much of my time grading work that was not written by my student. I don't have the time to grade AI.

Student: Why would I put forth more than minimal effort into this assignment when my instructor has a reputation for using AI detectors that are incorrect? Why not simply game this system so that I pass this class and move on?

Such interactions will likely increase in frequency until a coherent set of policies *and* practices emerge. To be adaptive, both policies and practices should encourage the best use-cases of AI to enhance education, rather than detract from it.

Notably, this also requires the EdTech sector to pose solutions, rather than play both sides. Much like arms dealers benefit if both sides of a conflict purchase their weapons, so too do EdTech (and big tech) companies benefit from designing "solutions" to problems that they themselves created in the name of innovation and efficiency.

The Erosion of Critical Thinking

One of the first imaginary giants that have emerged as GenAI tools have reached ubiquity in college and K12 classrooms is the notion that GenAI tools *necessarily* reduce students' capacity to be critical thinkers. Some of this is likely due to both the near-frictionless experience of using a GenAI tool, as well as the illusory cognition that is perpetuated by GenAI platforms themselves (e.g., language that tools are "thinking" rather than processing when they generate responses to queries).

An early study from Microsoft researchers and Carnegie Mellon researchers seemed to substantiate these claims, with authors concluding that "higher confidence in GenAI is associated with less critical thinking" (Lee, Sarkar, et al., 2025). This finding has echoed popular sentiment (e.g., Rosario, 2025) as well as anxieties over large-scale pilot projects (e.g., Duke University's partnership with OpenAI; Lin & Pinnameneni, 2025). Other scholarly work coined phrases like "metacognitive laziness" to define potential detriments to students due to increased dependence on AI assistance, undermining what we know to be good self-regulated learning behaviors that encourage metacognition (Fan et al., 2025).

Studies like this have a tendency to grab headlines because their core finding is interesting, yet the devil is always in the details. The first core limitation of the Lee, Sarkar, et al. (2025) study, for example, is that critical thinking as an outcome measure was self-reported. The challenges with self-report measures are that one never really knows what participants are thinking when they answer questions. As such, the educational psychology field has moved away from only relying on self-report measures (e.g., Fulmer & Frijters, 2009). The authors themselves acknowledge this, stating that "participants occasionally conflated reduced effort in using GenAI with reduced effort in critical thinking with GenAI."

Their view of critical thinking, moreover, is also narrowly defined as tasks that ensure "the objectives and quality of [participants'] work." Even Fan et al. (2025) who coined the term "metacognitive laziness" readily admit they did not directly measure "metacognitive laziness," and are speculating as to potential negative effects associated with GenAI use. I stress that both sets of authors do not overstate their claims, but studies like these feed into notions that GenAI tools are positioned to undermine students' critical thinking skills. The fact of the matter is that the science is still underway. My own work on the topic, for example, has shown that students use GenAI for a host of reasons, and their reasons are informed by their instructors (Macias & Aguilar, 2026).

Thus, the current evidence is murky, at best. Pence et al. (2024), for example, has shown that students may engage in *more* critical thinking as they correct errors made by GenAI models. Lee (2025) has also demonstrated that there are many reasons students use GenAI tools, not all of which are nefarious, and many of which can support adaptive educational processes. This is why the erosion of critical thinking at the hands of GenAI is an imagined monster—the current evidence simply does not support that assertion. Moreover, as should be obvious by this point in the book, any technology operates in a complex sociotechnical system that shapes what is and isn't possible.

Thus, the (AI-alarmist) fear that students may become overly reliant on GenAI for assignments, skipping essential learning processes such as problem-solving and analytical reasoning, is misplaced. Such a future will only occur if educators do not adapt, use, or otherwise acclimate to the capabilities of GenAI tools. AI-alarmists often argue that GenAI might undermine the development of critical thinking skills, especially in foundational subjects, but in so doing conflate automation with critical thinking.

In fact, the coming ubiquity of GenAI content requires us to expand our critical thinking, and as such creates an opportunity to use GenAI to push our students to critically evaluate generated content. Educators must first adapt and shift their instruction and assessments to accommodate the ubiquity of GenAI tools. This is not an easy task, but nor is it impossible.

Although the objects of critique may change, the act of critiquing and using critical thinking skills does not. What can be troublesome, however, is when educators do not adapt. Educators must first become critical evaluators of GenAI content themselves so that they can teach their students to do the same. Without doing so, a sort of dissonance between artifacts of critique and the instruction used to critique them can emerge. This, I suspect, is the cause of our anxiety with respect to losing critical thinking.

A key safeguard against students concluding that they can offload their cognition onto GenAI applications is by disabusing them of the notion that GenAI tools are "intelligent." It is essential to emphasize that the illusory cognitive capacity of GenAI applications is a function of deliberate design features. Why else would tools like ChatGPT bother conflating computation time with "thinking"? Without correcting this fundamental misconception, students may actually think that they are offloading their thinking onto GenAI applications that can "think" for them. In so doing, they both misunderstand GenAI and reduce their own cognition to output from a Synthetic Human Artifact Machine.

6

GenAI Fueled Equity?

Chapter Outline

Introduction

As the previous chapter showed, we would do well to not fall into the trap of AI-alarmism, as doing so precludes us from truly engaging with the affordances of GenAI in education. Similarly, however, we should attend to some of the core issues that surface when considering using GenAI in classrooms. To that end, this chapter pushes back on ideas that are most often promoted by AI-zealots. Usually, their ideas are overly optimistic and include claims that GenAI will bring about a new era of equity in education.

Although it is true that GenAI is positioned to help us do more with fewer resources, it is still unclear who these newly discovered efficiencies will benefit. As my work and the work of others suggest, benefits derived from GenAI use will likely be unevenly distributed (Kangwa et al., 2025; Xiu & Aguilar, 2026). It simply is not the case that the mere invention of new technologies ushers in prosperity; as resource allocation is a function of federal, state, and local policies, as well as the choices individuals make to enact (or ignore) such policies.

As always, the sociotechnical system matters. Ambitious claims of GenAI fueled prosperity by AI-zealots ignore the fact that inequities remain persistent, despite us living in what can arguably be considered the most productive era of human existence. In fact, it is not only feasible, but likely, that GenAI, under the right conditions, may exacerbate existing inequalities or even create new ones.

We do not have to go far to see how this might occur. We can go back less than ten years and examine the inequities that surfaced during the COVID-19 pandemic, an era in which technology was hailed as a way to revolutionize and reimagine education. Instead, learning losses and unequal access to educational tools highlighted the real-world limitations of technology-based solutions. At this point in the GenAI revolution, it is necessary to interrogate the core claims of AI-zealots, that is, more efficiency, greater personalization, and the potential to "level the playing field."

The Myth of GenAI as an Equalizer

If AI-alarmists think that GenAI technologies will usher in a world where all students are unable to think for themselves, then AI-zealots believe that GenAI will usher in a world where every student's educational experience will be personalized in powerful ways. This personalization at scale, the AI-zealot argues, will ensure that learning and academic gains will be all but guaranteed.

Initiatives like Alpha School, where teachers are largely replaced by GenAI, already hint at such attitudes (Salhotra & Rios, 2025). The argument is seductive: if GenAI tools can personalize experiences at a very granular level for each and every student with nothing more than a laptop or Chromebook, then why would we need teachers? Especially when teachers often have to teach to the needs of the "average" student? Such strategies seem outdated, and arguably leave kids who need more support behind, while simultaneously boring kids who have already mastered the content and require enrichment activities. This argument is somewhat overstated on my part, but it is not far off from the current discourse about GenAI.

I am willing to go out on a limb to predict that GenAI will not be a force that equalizes education in a way that removes the variability in what students experience. The fact of the matter is, those with more resources will get better and more powerful versions of whatever GenAI has to offer. Students with access to fewer resources will still get helpful tools, but they will be impoverished versions of the "premium" tools. We already see this happening with the off the shelf, "vanilla," GenAI tools which have limitations when compared to the paid versions (Lambert & Stevens, 2024).

I readily admit that such variation in experience is a necessary component to the economics of GenAI products. However, economic arguments for differing experiences are irrelevant when considering notions of equity. In fact, we already see variation happening in real time, with large systems such as Duke, California State Universities, and other large institutional bodies with bargaining power able to offer large pilot programs in collaboration with OpenAI and other AI companies (Lin & Pinnameneni, 2025; Barajas, 2025). Thus, not only will GenAI not usher in a new era of equity, it will instead create another dimension of *inequity* among students.

While it is common to hear that GenAI technological advancements will uplift marginalized communities (e.g., Goldstein, 2024; Li & Iacobelli, 2023), the fact of the matter is that while well-meaning, this argument ignores the fact that stark inequities persist despite us living in an era of unprecedented technological productivity. Thus, claims that GenAI will become a de facto equalizing force are historically misguided. Instead, GenAI-driven educational equity will only occur by advocating for broader access to new innovations.

When EdTech Didn't Deliver

EdTech has a storied history of creating innovative technologies that can be used by teachers and students alike. This includes what we would now consider basic tools like electronic encyclopedias (e.g., Derby & Richardson, 2001), games that help students learn math concepts (Young et al., 2012), and simple things like grammar and spell checkers. It also includes more novel technologies, such as cognitive tutors (Anderson et al., 1995), learning analytics applications (Lonn et al., 2015; Park & Jo, 2015), and learning management systems (e.g., Blackboard). GenAI tools are merely the newest entry in a long history of technologies developed for educators and students alike.

In Chapter 3 I discussed how the COVID-19 pandemic was a time when many believed technology would "revolutionize" or "reimagine" what education could be post-pandemic. Far from ushering in a new world of educational innovation and educational equity, the pandemic resulted in learning loss for many students and revealed major disparities in access to educational resources (Engzell et al., 2021; Polikoff & Silver, 2022).

It is tempting to argue that the pandemic was a unique time, and pandemic-era disruptions explain why the EdTech of the day failed to live up to its potential. This train of thought, however, is fundamentally incorrect because technology has never been the issue. When considering the entire sociotechnical system—of which technologies are merely one part—it becomes easier to see that any given technology will be unable to address systemic inequities, even when its potential seems high. This is because other aspects need to fall into place before a technology can make a positive difference.

Access to technology, for example, has always been a problem. It has also been a topic of study for decades. In the early 2000s, concerns over who had access to the internet and computers took center stage. It's interesting looking back, as discussions of the day centered on technologies that most of us take for granted. It is unsurprising, then, that data from the period shows that Latino communities had less access to computers, as they had less access to *many* resources (Matute, 2001). Low-income communities, moreover, had less access to the internet compared to their wealthier peers (Digital Divide Slugfest, 2002).

Gaps in computer access began as early as the first grade, and lack of access was more common among poorer schools (Judge et al., 2004). Work in this area showed that even when student-to-device ratios were even, "the social contexts of computer use differed, with low-SES schools affected by uneven human support networks" (Warschauer et al., 2004). This lends evidence to the fact that when it comes down to it, equity is more about resourcing the entire sociotechnical system than it is about enabling access to particular devices.

In the 2010s, we see a similar pattern emerge. News articles and scholars alike noted that disadvantaged students did not have access to computers relative to their more affluent peers (Pandolfo, 2012). Access to Wi-Fi internet was also seen as the "equity gap" of the day, and thus a potential lever to reduce inequities (Middleton & Chambers, 2010). Scholars who focused on studying digital equity gaps found that such gaps persisted despite lower costs of technology, as Warschauer and Matuchniak (2010) note:

> There is a widespread belief that the falling cost of computers and Internet access is rapidly narrowing a digital divide in U.S. society. However . . . gaps in home access to digital media are still substantial, and inequalities in technology usage and outcomes are even greater.

Fast forward another decade, and we see that *too much* access to technology was an indicator of disadvantage. Writers in the late 2010s, for example, lamented over the fact that wealthier children spent *less* time on screens relative to their low-income peers, and were thus "privileged" (Riley, 2018).

Regardless of era, advances in digital technologies seem doomed to spark the same old debate, with advocates of digital equity lamenting over gaps in access, training, and use of whichever new technology happens to be in vogue at the time. This leads to increased attention, and sometimes to increased access. Both fuel further debates and studies focused on understanding what positive impacts more access will bring. I have not been immune to these debates, as my recent work on the pandemic (i.e., Aguilar et al., 2022) and equity vis-à-vis learning analytics indicates (i.e., Aguilar, 2020b).

Like Sisyphus pushing a boulder up an incline only to have it fall again, new technologies renew the same tired debates and studies about the impacts associated with certain communities getting access to newer technologies. These debates make obvious and unhelpful points, such as the fact that low-income communities who do not get access to new technologies will be disadvantaged—as though they did not *begin* disadvantaged. This creates a loop of work that is focused on digital equity defined by lamentation and responses to it. The technologies themselves exist in a paradoxical state of being both the causes of, and solutions to, inequities that are being experienced at a given point in time.

GenAI technologies have taken center stage in the current debate. Many ask us to begin the Sisyphean task of pushing the rock of GenAI up an incline, never wondering why such efforts are fruitless. I find such tasks tiresome.

The answer to inequity, as I've mentioned elsewhere but will repeat here, is that we must take into account the entire context of where a technology operates. This includes (obviously) the technology itself, but further includes the people who would use it and the places where it would be used. The entire system matters, and it does not matter if millions of dollars are spent on providing a given technology to a user or community if the rest of the sociotechnical system is not addressed in equal parts.

The Double-Edged Sword of Personalization

What is "personalization," and why should we assume that it is a net-positive approach to instruction? In general, personalization has been used effectively to promote engagement (Tetzlaff et al., 2021). We see this most readily with social media technologies (Eg et al., 2023) and games (Paraschos, 2023), both of which are designed to create unique experiences for users and players, respectively. Conceptually this makes sense—I am more likely to stay engaged with a process, product, or platform that reflects my interests and/or parts of my personal identity.

This understanding of how personalization can lead to further engagement often leads us to think of it as a solution for disparities within education. A teacher attending to what a set of students knows, in order to give them tasks that are within reach, for example, is a type of personalization that helps students learn. Unfortunately, this familiar approach to personalization is difficult to achieve at scale (e.g., Gibbs, 2023; Subban et al., 2025; Stairs-Davenport, 2023). Consequently, when we think about the potential of GenAI technologies, we often think of personalization at scale.

We also "personalize" the way we interact with one another. The use of analogies to explain unfamiliar concepts, for example, is one way to personalize an interaction. Analogies seek to introduce unfamiliar concepts by linking them to known concepts—a process known as acclimation (Alexander, 2003, 2005).

When I explained LLMs earlier in this book I used the idea of an appliance that consumed recipes. This was a way for me to bridge what I know with what you may know—my way of trying to personalize your learning experience while reading this book. You likely use analogies in your own profession all the time. When there is a foreign concept to explain, one often looks for common ground to begin the conversation. It is an inherently human—and intelligent—thing to do.

There is a long history of personalization in EdTech. It is not unlike our own process in that it requires data from the user, which will then be used to personalize their experience with the EdTech tool. Colloquially, we often refer to this process by referring to "the algorithm." As I've stated elsewhere, there is nothing inherently special about algorithms. Suffice it to treat them like automated decision makers based on predetermined information. Educators make decisions in an "algorithmic" way all the time, especially when deciding when, where, and how to personalize academic content. Educators have simply internalized the rules that define their algorithmic decision-making processes.

In many ways, recent innovation in EdTech has focused on replicating what master educators already do. Thus, if we return to cognitive tutors, we see similar concepts at play. Once a cognitive tutor knows enough about a student, lessons can be personalized to ensure students engage with content at their level. This helps reduce frustration, and ideally keeps students in the zone of proximal development, that is, ensuring that struggles are productive and lead to deeper understanding (Vygotsky, 1978; Shabani, 2010).

Data-driven personalization, however, is not without its issues. For one, it is based on a set of inputs; if the inputs are incorrect, then the personalized experience will also be incorrect. When this occurs, personalization fails in the same way a suit tailored for my colleague (who is 5'9 and stout) will not fit my athletic 6'2" build. An ongoing challenge with personalization within EdTech and GenAI, however, is that there is often a lack of an "explicit pedagogical perspective" (e.g., Bartolomé et al., 2018). One has to know how to teach before an educational experience can be personalized. This is fundamentally different from encouraging engagement through personalized user experiences.

Unfortunately, personalization in EdTech is often constrained by behaviorist approaches to learning (see Watson, 2017 for a discussion on behaviorism). A behaviorist who uses operant conditioning, for example, seeks to reinforce behaviors through negative reinforcement, positive reinforcement, or punishment. Both negative and positive reinforcement seek to increase behaviors, either by adding a reward (positive reinforcement) or by removing a negative stimulus (negative reinforcement). Punishments, on the other hand, reduce the frequency of behaviors.

All behaviorist approaches to teaching myopically focus on the consequences of applied stimuli and ignore the inner worlds of the learner. EdTech is often limited to behaviorist approaches because the data gathered is constrained to what a user *does* with a specific technology. This includes keystrokes, clicks, eye-gaze, and so on. It is a limited way to approach the learner because we are more than the sum of our behaviors.

That is why the human element matters. Teachers can notice body language, intonation of speech, and a host of other behaviors (e.g., Andersen et al., 1985). They can also ask students questions that might seem out of place, but serve a purpose. In short, they acknowledge the multitude of dimensions of the learning experience because they see their students as full human beings with rich inner worlds that are not always reflected in outward behaviors.

Technology-driven approaches to personalization cannot attend to students' humanity nearly as well. Thus, despite popular notions to the contrary, personalization with Edtech is actually quite difficult (FitzGerald et al., 2018). Behaviorist approaches require strict dichotomies, that is, behaviors to encourage vs. behaviors to discourage—a "1" and a "0." This is easy enough when sought-after behaviors are easily captured. Amazon knows they succeeded, for example, if I buy something. Recording an instance of learning *the moment it happens* is not possible. We instead use proxies for learning.

That said, when personalization works, it works well and can lead to academic gains (Major et al., 2021). GenAI approaches to personalization are also more nimble than traditional approaches. However, those who suggest that GenAI can help resolve some of the challenges with respect to personalization would do well to recall that GenAI technologies have a way of creating homogeneity; "the indiscriminate use of GenAI risks homogenising learners' performance and creativity, limiting the discovery of their potential" (Laak et al., 2024).

GenAI's promises of personalized learning are a double-edged sword. While it is true that personalization may help students receive more targeted educational experiences, such personalization may ironically come at the cost of less creativity. They also might lead to *less* personalized attention by teachers, especially if popular models to deploy GenAI end up increasing student-teacher ratios.

AI and Ethics: What's Really at Stake

When we discuss inequity and how GenAI might affect groups differently, what we're often talking about is *ethics*. It's worth lingering on ethics for a moment, but not in a way that asks questions that are both important and have obvious answers, such as:

- **Question**: Will AI replace teachers?
- **Answer**: No, but that won't stop folks from trying.
- **Question**: Which groups will get to use the "best" AI?
- **Answer**: Those with money, connections, or (likely) both.
- **Question:** Who will make the decisions about what's best for us with regard to AI use?
- **Answer**: In the United States, those in power, and (currently) the private sector, as the US federal government has ceded responsibility (The White House, 2025b).
- **Question:** Will AI wreak havoc on the world?
- **Answer:** Yes and no. Yes in predictable ways and among predictable communities. Havoc—also known as disruption—will not happen in broad strokes and instead build as little failures that amount to large ones, over time.

I could keep going, but hypotheticals like the ones above are limited. They are bound in time, and both the question and answers are based on potentially unsurfaced ethical positions. Whether or not we know it, we all have ethical sensibilities that drive how we interpret what is or isn't ethical. Note: I do not mean anything as blunt as religion, as religions are structures built on top of ethical positions that can be uncovered by interrogating some of their core positions. Religions *enact* ethics and encourage those actions within communities and through rituals.

How then, might we begin to uncover our own ethical presuppositions and push others to do the same? One approach is to conduct a classic thought experiment: the Trolley Problem (Thomson, 1976). If you have ever taken an introductory philosophy class, there is a very strong chance you have been posed this problem. The simple version of it is as follows.

Imagine you are on a road and approach a set of tracks that fork in two directions. Thus, when a train travels down the tracks, it will travel down one of the two forks. Disturbingly, as you look down the tracks, you see that there are five people tied up, unable to move. On the other set of tracks, there is only one person tied up, unable to move. Neither set can communicate with you or each other.

Unfortunately, there is also a train that is headed toward the five people who are tied up! You know that if you do nothing, the train will run over and kill them. It is at this moment that you also see a lever. You know that if you pull that lever you can divert the train so that instead of running over five people, it gets diverted to the other set of tracks. Sadly, this means that it would run over the *other* person who is tied up.

Thus, your *only* two options in this thought experiment are:

1) Do nothing; the train kills the five people on the main track, or
2) Pull the lever, and divert the train to the other set of tracks, where it will kill one person.

Take a moment and think about what you would do in this situation *and why you would do it.* It's a tough question, and your answer—and the debate leading to it—uncovers your ethical beliefs about what constitutes an ethical choice. Do you act and pull the lever, saving five people at the expense of directly causing the death of another person, or do you choose to do nothing? The core of this problem, and why it's posed so often, is that it highlights the struggle between two types of ethical systems: Consequentialism and Deontology.

Consequentialists care about *consequences*, and are thus concerned with following the causal chain of events to determine the correct course of action. Thus, when one is working within a consequentialist framework, one endorses the notion that what is "ethical" is defined as actions, policies, and so on, that maximize overall happiness, or "good."

So, if you pulled the lever, then you acted morally because you believe that you saved five lives *at the expense* of one life. Consequentialism is primarily concerned with this moral calculus because ethical actions are a result of calculating outcomes resulting from choices made. This math is to ensure that good outcomes are maximized. Given any hard choice, the consequentialist will game out the results and act accordingly. In this case, preserving life is the good to be maximized, so the choice is simple: five lives saved are greater than one life lost. This ethical system underpins John Stuart Mill's *Utilitarianism* (1863/2016).

A deontologist, however, operates from an entirely different premise; one where ethical acts are derived from following a set of universal moral rules, such as "it is wrong to intentionally kill someone." At the core of deontological ethics, then, is coming up with a set of rules that can guide action, as there is no reason to look at consequences to the degree that a consequentialist might. Immanuel Kant's "Categorical Imperatives," (Kant, 1998/1785) are one such example, though there are many.

What matters for this discussion is that the deontologist checks actions against a pre-determined set of rules, and only acts if they do not violate said rules. In our thought experiment, the deontologist would choose to do nothing, because by acting they would be *causing* death, which is unethical. This position would necessarily result in the death of five individuals instead of one, and would be seen as the moral choice.

I've posed this thought experiment many times during talks I've given around the country. No matter where I give this talk, I am always surprised by the breakdown in the audience. It's never quite 50/50. Yet, there is enough of a mix to suggest different sets of core values—or core ethical stances—that may not have surfaced in day-to-day professional interactions.

For example, about 30 percent of my audience in a Midwestern university sided with a consequentialist choice, while only 5 percent of a similarly sized audience in a Southern California mountain community did the same (Aguilar, 2025). Regardless of the outcome, I always tell my audience the same thing: it does not matter what choice you made, what matters is having a deep understanding of the reasons you used to make it. Being able to answer those second-order questions is what matters the most, as they force us to not only take positions but understand our core values and ethical presuppositions.

At this point you may be asking yourself, "why does any of this matter when it comes to GenAI?" It matters because all one needs to do is change the thought experiment. Here are two ethical positions based on both deontology and consequentialist positions:

> **Deontologist:** GenAI should be designed and deployed in ways that respect **human autonomy**. This can involve clear opt-in/opt-out features, **transparency** about how the AI is making decisions, and options for human review or override of AI decisions. Government regulation can help incentivize and police compliance to ensure innovation does not disrupt the core principles of human autonomy and transparency.
>
> **Consequentialist:** Generative AI can increase productivity by **automating** routine tasks, answering questions, offering suggestions, and more. This can lead to **improved efficiency** in various sectors such as business, healthcare, education, and others. AI development should be left in the hands of the private sector, which is best positioned to find optimal pathways for GenAI development and deployment.

Importantly, neither of the above positions are *necessarily* in opposition to one another, as each is concerned with its own set of ethical imperatives. The deontologist sees GenAI development as tightly coupled with implications for individuals. They might think, for example, that in a world where automated decisions become the norm, it becomes increasingly likely that important decisions will be made by GenAI, instead of by people.

We saw inklings of this with Elon Musk's DOGE (Demirjian & Nehamas, 2025), however other sectors are experimenting with things like AI dynamic pricing and other systems that effectively make human input unnecessary (Hyde, 2025). Coupled with transparency, the deontologist position seeks to set rules that help buttress, rather than undermine, individual choices. The consequentialist, on the other hand, sees GenAI as enabling more productivity—which will enable individuals to do more with less. Teachers could, for example, give students more individualized attention if they were unburdened by administrative tasks.

The tricky thing, however, is that thought experiments are too simple. They do not address nuance, such as communities whose members may hold different positions about the same topic. Recent work of mine showed, for example, that male versus female teachers held different ethical positions about GenAI relative to each other (Aguilar & Wang, 2024). Those differences can cause tension, which can in turn lead to inaction when it comes to determining when GenAI use should be encouraged or discouraged.

Thought experiments also become more complex when one considers second and third order effects. Protecting transparency and autonomy, for example, might create more bureaucratic hurdles to develop newer technologies. While slower can indeed be better, there is no guarantee of that. Similarly, the push for efficiency is often at the cost of human involvement, which can and has interrupted human lives and livelihoods.

Consequently, thought experiments are limited in terms of practical application. Eventually, the rubber meets the road, and we are forced to contend with the circumstances and realities that are bound in time and place. That said, they are not useless; they are essential for us to surface our underlying ethical presuppositions so we can have clear and authentic discussions about what matters to *us* and *why*, while also leaving room for others to do the same.

Without those conversations, we can often reduce those who disagree with us in ways that are unproductive. We can reduce individuals to positions they might not have carefully interrogated. That sort of disagreement leads to both incoherence and intractability—two things we should avoid when developing rules and norms around GenAI's use in educational settings.

7

GenAI and K12

Chapter Outline

Introduction

There are many potential consequences to using GenAI tools in K12 settings. It could be that GenAI tools enable teachers to do more with less. Changes to assignments, assessments, and student engagement, moreover, will continue to evolve as a result of GenAI. What will change, and how fast it will change, is not fully known. Indeed, the study of potential changes to pedagogy, student achievement, and student engagement is an active area of study within the academic community.

What is clear, however, is that there are at least three groups of stakeholders that we should attend to when discussing the consequences of GenAI tool use in K12 settings: administrators, teachers, and students. Each group will experience both potential benefits and challenges as GenAI is integrated into the classroom. Administrators will likely be attracted to GenAI tools due to their promise of increased efficiency. Teachers might gravitate toward GenAI tools so that they can help their students learn in more personalized ways. Students, for their part, will find their own uses for GenAI, though perhaps in ways that undermine learning.

My approach to discussing GenAI's impact on K12 will be to draw on events that have already occurred. This includes both well-known challenges like Los Angeles Unified School District's (LAUSD) failure to launch a large GenAI initiative, to less known successes like Santa Ana Unified's "AI Compass." Although such cases are illustrative of potential patterns of GenAI adoption and development, they are not exhaustive. Instead, they invite us to consider possibilities.

A theme that will emerge, however, is that we would do well to be wary of a myopic administrative focus on doing more with less. Education is a community effort, and a focus on efficiency can undermine the community-based values that should guide decisions about GenAI's inclusion or exclusion. Moreover, an efficiency-driven mindset that prioritizes return on investment (ROI) over the needs of the people in our educational systems is destined to lead to more disparities.

District-level decisions aside, teachers stand to benefit from AI by offloading routine tasks, such as grading or lesson planning, allowing them to focus more on building relationships with students. However, this introduces a tension between relying on GenAI tools and maintaining the human connection necessary for understanding students on a deeper level. Further, there is the possibility that AI-zealots who wish to innovate will talk themselves out of needing teachers at all. Such programs are already in development or active use (Salhotra & Rios, 2025).

For students, there are many potential uses of GenAI tools. They can, for example, offload seemingly tedious tasks, such as the deep reading of texts. They can also use GenAI to write on topics they do not feel compelled to engage with. Both types of GenAI use enable superficial engagement and can also create an environment that discourages students from trying and failing, which is an important part of learning.

If students rely on GenAI to assist them with academic tasks, they may lose the ability to engage deeply with material. Over time, this would affect their long-term knowledge retention and potentially lead to a decline in confidence. Using GenAI as a peer or tutor among younger students may also lead to unanticipated second-order effects, such as discouraging students from engaging with their peers. This is troublesome, as peer connections coupled with a sense of belonging are necessary components to creating healthy learning environments (Slaten et al., 2016; Ibarra, 2022).

In short, there is a world of possibilities for administrators, teachers, and students. While I cannot anticipate all possible worlds with respect to GenAI use, I can still give you a few places to start. Thus, we begin with the specter of efficiency.

Administrative Efficiency, a Wolf in Sheep's Clothing

But first, let's take a quick detour and talk about steak. I don't know about you, but I like some marbling in my ribeye steak. It tastes delicious. What is a lean ribeye without marbling? Culinary garbage. I liken my enjoyment of a well-marbled ribeye to the idea that sometimes education isn't *lean*. It's complex and inefficient. It's a ribeye steak. Too often, AI-zealots in education seek the most efficient path at the expense of "inefficient" processes that can inspire students in unanticipated ways. I can only assume that such AI-zealots also eat their steaks well-done and devoid of flavor. (Who am I kidding? They probably drink protein shakes to "maintain efficiency.")

Jokes aside, I am referring, of course, to the notion that GenAI will make education more efficient. One of the most alluring aspects of GenAI in K12 spaces is the notion that teachers, administrators, and staff can "increase efficiency." Administrators may, for example, be drawn to GenAI technologies for their supposed ability to increase productivity and reduce costs.

Teachers may find that they can spend less time doing paperwork, grading, creating slides for class, and so on, in order to increase the one-on-one time they can devote to the students in their classrooms. Such efforts are well intentioned. After all, if everyone has more time, then why wouldn't they be able to spend more time on what "matters"?

There are many examples of how one might achieve this. Santa Ana Unified School District (SAUSD), located in Southern California, for example, has outlined an ambitious plan for using GenAI to offload some administrative tasks. Documents like handbooks, policies, and so on, are often dense and not deeply understood by everyone in an organization.

SAUSD addressed this challenge by creating their own personalized chatbot through ChatGPT and using district documents to contextualize responses (Santa Ana Unified School District, 2024). Thus, staff, teachers, and administrators alike could simply "have a conversation" with their chatbot in order to answer policy-related questions.

Use-cases like this are somewhat innocuous and helpful when thinking about what's possible with GenAI in educational settings. Notably, however, SAUSD still had to ensure that the documents uploaded did not contain sensitive information. They also put in place oversight to ensure that the chatbot did not provide erroneous information to queries. This latter aspect is where efficiency might begin to break down. Often GenAI's mistakes are innocuous or amusing, other times they can introduce legal liability. Having to provide constant oversight of GenAI output, then, can actually *reduce* efficiency.

That is why I have grown to dislike the word "efficiency" as applied to GenAI's place in education. Efficiency has a way of reducing the salient dimensions of a context in ways that can impoverish the entire experience. To illustrate what I mean by this, I'll briefly touch on one of my hobbies: tabletop wargaming. (Don't worry, I will not recount the entire history of Warhammer 40,000—but maybe give it a read on your own.)

A player's goal in wargaming is simple, marshal a field of troops in order to defeat your enemy based on the scenario you've both decided to play together. "Troops" in this world are little plastic soldiers that one might spend hours painting or leave as bare plastic. Aesthetic choices are fun but do not impact the game. Instead, *which* troops you choose and what kind of equipment each troop has matters. Although the choices one makes are constrained (e.g., troops need to be in the same army, and a fielded army has size constraints), it can feel like there are an infinite number of options. This is what makes the game fun—options leading to unintended consequences.

There are, however, those who play in order to win at all costs. They are referred to by the pejorative term of "min-maxers." The idea behind min-maxing is simple, find the *minimum* set of circumstances that *maximizes* a desirable outcome. In war gaming, this desirable outcome is finding the combination of troop configurations that enable victory, even if this means fielding units that have rules known to make the game unfun for the other player. Playing against min-maxers is a chore because they treat the experience like an equation to be solved, rather than a communal experience between two people who have the same interests.

Min-maxing in education has similar problems. Efficiency, by definition, requires reducing dimensions in order to pick what one wants to streamline. This can lead to a reduction in an experience in order to find the shortest path to a desirable outcome. With SAUSD, for example, it is entirely possible to argue that once the GenAI system is dialed in, a reduction in support staff is warranted because the same amount of work can be done with less labor. To my knowledge, SAUSD did not reduce their workforce thanks to GenAI, but such arguments are common both within and outside of the education community.

Labor is, after all, one of the more expensive parts of any budget; people are "expensive," so it stands to reason that the most efficient system will minimize the number of personnel needed to obtain a desirable outcome. We used to bristle at the idea that teachers were expendable. With the advent of GenAI tools, however, that seems to be changing. There are already schools experimenting with "teacher-lite" approaches, where students spend much of their time engaged with GenAI systems while an adult "guide" (not teacher) facilitates the process (Salhotra & Rios, 2025).

One argument of such models is that they prepare students for a future where using GenAI is the norm. Yet, I have not heard predictions of a future where most of us will not engage with our fellow human beings to accomplish a task. Instead, implicit in these models is the notion of efficiency—of doing more with less. Within these models lies a fetishization of efficiency that seeks to maximize a chosen outcome. Unfortunately, such models prioritize metrics over human-centered approaches to education. If given a choice, would you give your child a GenAI tutor or a well-trained human tutor? It is worth sitting with your answer and considering your reasons behind it.

AI-zealots seek to reduce education to an input-output machine: input child, output child who knows more about, science, technology, or whichever subject the AI-zealot wants to maximise. Yet, this is not the primary purpose of education. Education is as much about building relationships with other learners as it is about learning specific content. Thus, while doing more with less is appealing, it may come at the cost of the community experiences that schools are meant to foster.

Why Belonging and Community Matter

Most learning environments are inherently social. When we attend educational institutions (e.g., schools, colleges), for example, we generally do so with others who also seek to learn. Even asynchronous activities such as watching YouTube videos have built-in social components that affect learning (Chen, 2025). It is unsurprising, then, that educational psychology research has studied the effects of belonging on learning for decades.

The need to belong is powerful and is an essential component of any learning environment and has been formalized by theories such as Self-Determination Theory (SDT; Ryan & Deci, 2002; Deci & Ryan, 2012). SDT posits that belonging is an essential component of academic motivation. If we do not feel a sense of belonging, we may not wish to engage. Think of a time when you felt out of place relative to your peers. In such a case, you likely attended to your own feelings rather than the learning task at hand. That is why, along with competence and autonomy, belonging is a crucial component of SDT's tripartite theory of motivation.

There are many school-level factors that predict students' sense of belonging, such as classroom climate, opportunities for recreation, socializing spaces, and the size of schools (Slaten et al., 2016). At the core of fostering a sense of belonging is enabling students to feel a sense of acceptance with regard to a larger community as well as the subject matter the community is focused on learning (e.g., math). Work in this area has shown that students' feelings of acceptance drive notions of belonging (Osterman, 2000), and special populations of students, such as English Language Learners (ELL) and students with disabilities both benefit from learning environments that foster a sense of belonging (Ibarra, 2022; Jenkinson, 2000).

Belonging is so essential to students' learning that there have been many interventions to improve it, with successful ones focused on "[promoting] positive interactions between students and between school staff and students" (Allen et al., 2022). Teachers play a central role in such interventions, as they curate classroom cultures that help their students feel a sense of belonging. Thus, schools where positive behaviors are enabled through teacher interventions have been shown to help students feel a greater sense of belonging (Nix et al., 2022).

A common argument for GenAI's integration into schools is that they will ease teachers' workloads by automating mundane tasks, allowing them to focus more on building relationships with students. This would, the argument goes, help with students' sense of belonging. Such arguments harken back to my earlier discussion about personalization (Chapter 6).

It seems valid that if the right tasks are offloaded onto GenAI tools, then teachers themselves will have more time to be leaders of learning communities, as they would not have to focus on other administrative tasks. Thus, eliminating admin or bookkeeping distractions would, hypothetically, give teachers the bandwidth to build stronger relationships with their students and attend to student peer group dynamics. Yet, teachers' views on using GenAI to help them become better teachers are mixed and indicate that there is more complexity than we might presuppose (Prilop et al., 2025).

Aside from empowering teachers, there are those who would use GenAI technologies *themselves* as instruments that help increase students' sense of belonging. This includes using GenAI tools as anthropomorphized "peers." It also includes personalizing learning resources (e.g., assignments) so that students feel more connected to them. Teachers would do well to be suspicious of the former use-case while being mindful not to overuse the latter.

Even advocates of this latter view recognize its limitations; for example, "[GenAI] should not be an aid to replace human connection but as an assistive tool to promote connectedness with other humans, places, and things" (Pani et al., 2024). Still, early work has shown that the latter use-case, that is, generating content to better match students' interests, can indeed enable students to feel greater affinity toward specific subjects (e.g., math), which further encourages them to feel a part of a learning community focused on that subject (Norberg et al., 2025).

As with the integration of all educational technologies, the burden of how to implement such technologies will fall on teachers. They will be ultimately responsible for delicately balancing using GenAI to enhance their own productivity while ensuring that technology does not depersonalize the learning process for their students. As the final arbiters of the learning tasks their students experience, teachers will shape what "GenAI" integration means in their local contexts. In this case, they will shape their own localized sociotechnical system while attending to external constraints.

GenAI and Teacher-Student Ratios

GenAI tools are already being used by teachers, students, and administrators. The effects of such use are currently being studied, as are the attitudes and perceptions of those who use—or are subjected to—GenAI tools. Although the literature in this area is nascent and evolving (read: no one knows or agrees on anything yet), what is already clear is that arguments for how GenAI will affect K12 classrooms, with respect to teacher-student ratios and classroom size, have been paradoxical.

On the one hand, there have been advocates who suggest that GenAI technologies will help teachers save time by streamlining administrative burdens, enabling them to give more attention to their students. Such advocates suggest that this will make classrooms feel smaller because teachers who use AI will net more time for each student as their administrative burdens are offloaded to GenAI (e.g., Keppler et al., 2025; Klopfer et al., 2024; Tongchai & Malakul, 2025).

On the other hand, dissent about GenAI in education has focused on ways that GenAI's use will inevitably lead to students entering classrooms with more students per teacher. After all, if teachers can do more with less, then why wouldn't that also mean they can teach more students? We might even consider getting rid of teachers altogether and replacing them with caretakers, thereby leaving all pedagogical decisions to GenAI tools. Those who hold this view imagine a world where large classrooms are filled with students in front of screens, effectively depersonalizing the classroom experience.

As with other educational technologies, the truth of what will occur will be muddy and locally defined. In short, both of the above scenarios will happen—or neither will happen, depending on the choices that local educators make. Thus, it is currently unclear how GenAI's integration into classrooms will disrupt traditional teacher-student ratios.

We have cause to worry and push back against arguments that would reduce the teaching workforce, as the research on teachers' positive impact on student outcomes is clear. We know, for example, that lower student-teacher ratios can lead to improved academic outcomes for students (Schwartz et al., 2012). We also know that the quality of teachers has always mattered for helping students master content (Darling-Hammond, 2000). Overall, smaller class sizes tend to benefit students, but maintaining them is often costly, and there is no set formula for how small a class needs to be in order to reap the benefits (e.g., Ehrenberg et al., 2001; Chingos, 2013).

Although we do not know what effects the use of GenAI tools will have on students, we *do* know that giving teachers more time to teach is helpful and can help students learn better and more deeply. When teachers have more time to engage with their students in dialogue, for example, we know that students tend to engage more deeply with content (Howe et al., 2019).

This is an intuitive finding—when teachers have more time to pay attention to students under their professional care, they can bring more of their experience to bear when interacting with any given student. Recent evidence also suggests that more technology-forward approaches, such as blended learning (where students consume direct instruction asynchronously) can support student learning through similar mechanisms (Li & Wang, 2022).

Thus, the base of evidence is clear: teachers make a difference, and it is generally a good idea to give teachers more time to hone their craft. This is, however, not the same as having teachers outsource their craft to GenAI tools. This is a key distinction, as there is an assumption among those who propose the affordances of GenAI that implicitly undervalues the role of living, breathing educators in the room.

The claim that GenAI tools will make certain teaching behaviors obsolete and/or increase efficiency such that class sizes can justifiably *grow* is based on faulty logic. Teachers are more than "content creators" who deliver educational content to students under their care. They are bridges of knowledge, yes, but they are also arbiters of disputes among students, and help students develop into persons who have knowledge (Moje, 1996).

As technology advances, there is a risk that schools will use GenAI to increase student-teacher ratios, potentially limiting the one-on-one attention students receive, which could adversely affect learning outcomes. This should be avoided until we better understand all of the downstream implications such changes would cause.

Students and the Trade-Offs of AI-Enhanced Learning

This brings us to the student experience. Regardless of the era, students are always subjected to the decisions of teachers and administrators. While students have agency within this system, the truth of the matter is that students are at the mercy of others' decisions. Teachers and administrators define what students' school days look like.

Unfortunately, it is too early to describe the systemic impact of GenAI use on K12 students. Although work in this area is increasing in pace and frequency, the fact of the matter is that all studies with respect to GenAI have a shelf-life that is tied to the version of the GenAI tool being investigated. A study focused on the impacts of ChatGPT 3.0, for example, may be interesting to academics, but will have limited insights into what students of today are experiencing.

Current work has focused on the prevalence of GenAI tool use among students. Yet, even then, it is unclear exactly how pervasive GenAI use is among K12 students, though we do know that use has increased over time (Bueie et al., 2025). Moreover, while much work in this area has focused on plagiarism detection and prevention, it seems clear that GenAI tools can have positive effects on student learning when used properly—though such effects shift as a function of educational context (Liu et al., 2025).

Thus, while GenAI tools have been shown to help students complete tasks faster, there is a risk that they will not fully engage with, or retain, underlying concepts (Lee, 2025; Fan et al., 2025). As students turn to GenAI to help with more tasks, they might begin to question their own competence and expertise, leading to a potential decline in their ability to learn deeply and retain long-term knowledge. With regard to writing, for example, students have been shown to not always know how to balance GenAI use to remain authentic in reflective writing; they have also struggled with managing feelings of guilt over using GenAI tools (Chan et al., 2025).

Students have also been shown to rely on GenAI use when posing questions and evaluating answers (Abdelghani et al., 2025). This may be because current generation GenAI technologies are somewhat unruly and require more expertise to use effectively. Work in this area has shown that GenAI output often includes superfluous information that is long and ignores constraints imposed by students (Ohsaki & Matsukawa, 2025). When GenAI tools are positioned as teaching assistants, students can personify them in ways that teachers should be mindful of, as students have been shown to apply subjective characteristics to GenAI TAs, including considering them (less capable) peers. Though the effects of such personification, while technically incorrect and ethically complicated, have still been shown to lead to students' increased elaboration strategies (Song et al., 2024).

Thus, it is important to emphasize that students are not passive actors in their learning environments. Although the work in this area is nascent and complex, this complexity is also understood by students themselves. Studies in this area indicate that students understand that they are responsible for what they learn, and as such know that GenAI use is not always preferable to completing tasks independently (Adisa & Adefisayo, 2025). Students are also aware of the ethical concerns with GenAI use, and when asked to participate have centered concerns over combating bias and misinformation (Pu et al., 2025).

There are no "rules of thumb" that will always be true when it comes to students' use of GenAI tools. Each iteration of GenAI will be different from its previous version, and each will be integrated into unique learning environments that are shaped by the individuals in it, as well as the policies that govern it (i.e., the sociotechnical system). This is why it is essential for teachers to become familiar with the range of possibilities; students will need guidance from their teachers in order to leverage the positive uses of GenAI while avoiding negative use-cases.

8

GenAI and Higher Ed

Chapter Outline

Introduction

The rise of GenAI tools has been tightly coupled with higher education. This is partially because GenAI has been marketed to college students (Field, 2025), but marketing alone does not explain the impact of GenAI in college classrooms. Whether faculty like it or not, college students find GenAI tools useful. Thus, GenAI tools like Open AI's ChatGPT have become nearly ubiquitous among colleges and universities at a record pace.

GenAI has been criticized by faculty, as they fear what GenAI tool use will do to students' long-term ability to master content. Administrators, for their part, often find themselves caught in the middle. Many are in the unenviable position of wishing to ensure that faculty maintain academic freedom, while also pushing their institutions to accommodate the changes that have resulted from GenAI use among students (Dubois, 2024; Johnson et al., 2024).

Some university leaders have also argued that adopting GenAI is necessary for the survival of their institution, while others see it as another way to innovate and capture market share as students seek cutting-edge training for the workforce (Gilreath, 2025). While the word "crisis" is likely too strong to describe GenAI's impact on colleges and universities, it is not wholly incorrect to refer to what is happening as crisis-like. All post-secondary institutions were caught flat-footed when it came to adapting their instructional models to a world where students could generate synthetic human language and pass it off as their own.

This rapid change has resulted in a sense of anxiety among faculty and administrators. Initially, feelings of unease were driven by the shock of what GenAI tools could accomplish. Unfortunately, those feelings were further compounded by the fact that GenAI's capabilities evolve at a pace that is impossible to plan for. Thus, post-secondary institutions are left with two difficult tasks.

First, they must plan for the shifting sands of GenAI in order to ensure that academic rigor is maintained. Second, they must still be mindful that the world outside of academia faces similar challenges that have disrupted college students' ability to land entry-level jobs. Thus, an unsteady job market that has been disrupted by GenAI creates a feedback loop. This loop, in turn, causes a sense of urgency among college faculty, administrators, students, and parents. If GenAI is the future of expertise, some might argue, why would post-secondary degrees be worth the investment?

This chapter will not answer that question directly, as I take it as a presupposition that post-secondary education is necessary for an informed citizenry capable of both engaging and contributing to their communities. Knowledge helps us *do* things, and colleges and universities are purpose-built to help us learn what is necessary to maintain our ability to both understand the world around us and contribute to it.

That is why this chapter focuses on helping those in post-secondary institutions avoid the pitfalls of both AI-zealotry and AI-alarmism. GenAI technologies are useful for everyone who wishes to learn, but only if one treats them as tools for learning. All tools have inherent affordances and limitations that shape how we should use them.

Consequently, I argue for a moderate position that does not overcorrect for shifting markets and technologies. Rather than "reimagine" or "revolutionize" college education, post-secondary institutions should double-down on what they already do well. Although one might see this as a "back to basics" approach, I suspect that we are well beyond the days of blue book exams, oral exams, and the like. Instead, a hybrid approach that honors the history of a liberal arts education, while embracing the capabilities of GenAI technologies, is needed. This requires a steady, pragmatic approach that does not overreact to perceived threats or opportunities.

AI's Impact on Higher Education

To be pragmatic, we must first acknowledge (even begrudgingly) that GenAI tools will change much of the day-to-day operations of post-secondary institutions. Pragmatism also precludes us from being enticed by either of the extremes advocated by AI-zealots or AI-alarmists. We would do well to avoid thinking of changes that will "reimagine" or "revolutionize" colleges and universities. Instead, the process of GenAI tool integration will be defined by a gradual acclimation that will feel abrupt for some and slow for others.

During this process, post-secondary institutions will retain their mission of educating students so that they can learn a core set of skills, earn degrees, and enter the workforce. These skills, moreover, will serve them throughout their personal and professional lives. The core challenge for faculty and administrators, then, is determining *how* that will happen. Which GenAI tools will be brought to bear to accomplish the educational mission of each institution, and how will their use be evaluated?

Even before the explosion of GenAI, colleges and universities were already users of emerging technologies intended to both streamline operations and help students succeed. Many institutions experimented with "algorithmic decision making," that is, making decisions with limited human input. Occasionally, students found such processes fairer than the status quo (Marcinkowski et al., 2020; Chai et al., 2024).

Much of this work was conducted under the moniker of "learning analytics," which concerned itself with using large data sets that document student behaviors as they use educational technologies like learning management systems (LMSs). The idea behind learning analytics is to use data to better understand students' academic behaviors and potentially predict when students are at risk of academic failure or struggle. The effects of learning analytics applications were studied by myself and others (e.g., Lonn et al., 2015; Aguilar et al., 2021). It was common to see learning analytics as a way to increase positive outcomes for students. The more we know about students' use of EdTech, the argument goes, the better we can statistically model study behaviors.

The insights gained from such analyses led to many interventions intended to help students succeed in the face of challenges (Aguilar, 2018). Learning analytics interventions included those focused on personalization and evaluation (Leitner et al., 2017), and those aiming to understand students' individual experiences (Viberg et al., 2018). The field of learning analytics, in some ways, can be considered a prologue to what is happening today in colleges and universities across the world. Thus, the adoption of learning analytics driven approaches is one reason that the rapid growth of GenAI tools, while disruptive, has not been as chaotic as we might imagine.

Predictably, staff and faculty have different attitudes toward GenAI integration into their professional lives. Attitudes range from supportive to hesitant and resigned (Amani et al., 2023). Approaches by large teaching institutions, such as the Calforina State University system, show that training of staff and faculty over time enables more awareness and use. This does not, however, eliminate concerns over the ethical use of GenAI or concerns about how GenAI tool use might negatively affect student creativity (Dabirian et al., 2025).

On the student side, opinions are diverse, with some students reporting feelings of discomfort if GenAI is used to evaluate their well-being or grade them. Yet, students themselves have been shown to be comfortable with using GenAI tools (Rodway & Schepman, 2023). On the instructional side, the large language models that drive GenAI applications have been adapted to promote positive student study habits and reduce AI hallucinations (e.g., Qian et al., 2025). Other work has shown that AI can be used as a tool that supports educator feedback (e.g., Li et al., 2025c).

In short, there is no single approach or a common set of worries that define GenAI tool use in post-secondary settings. It is nonetheless clear, however, that GenAI will shape higher education, not through revolution, but through integration. Some of these changes will be gradual, while others will be abrupt and disruptive. Regardless of the pace of change, GenAI tool use is poised to affect teaching and administration back office duties.

None of these changes will fundamentally reimagine higher education, however. Instead, current patterns of GenAI tool use and adoption suggest a clear course of action. Professionals in post-secondary settings should engage with GenAI thoughtfully, recognizing both the opportunities and risks its use brings. Understanding the student voice is equally essential, as students share concerns about GenAI use. These concerns mirror broader societal anxieties about the role of GenAI in reshaping the workforce and human development.

The Fallacy of Banning AI in Education

It used to be that plagiarism was something to look out for, but recent developments have made plagiarism a thing of the past, as students are able to generate synthetic language that can be used in place of their own written sense-making. Thus, when GenAI technologies first became popular, initial reactions discussed potentially "banning" the use of GenAI tools. In practice, institutional bans were uncommon, and most post-secondary institutions left the final decision of whether or not GenAI tool use was allowed up to individual instructors (Gecker, 2023).

When bans do occur at the course level, however, they are more in spirit than in practice, as "AI detection" technologies are fallible (Zhou, 2023). This makes enforcing bans cumbersome, since the only sure-fire way to enforce them is to trust that students will abide by the ban—and turn themselves in if they break it. The obvious consequence of such policies is the undisclosed and confusing use of GenAI tools (e.g., Adnin et al., 2025). That is why "student compliance" approaches have been generally found to be ineffective (Corbin et al., 2025).

Overall, it seems clear that banning GenAI from higher education is neither feasible nor desirable, which is probably why few argue for outright bans. Instead, the debates about GenAI's place in post-secondary institutions have focused on ways to mitigate cheating on assessments, for example, by returning to in-person written or oral exams (Fenton, 2024). Discussions around the topic have also included polemic pieces that push back against industry hype while wishing to safeguard critical thinking and expertise (e.g., Guest et al., 2025). Such arguments seek to limit the use of GenAI tools and further argue that restrictive policies can be morally justified under limited circumstances (e.g., de Fine Licht, 2024). All discussions in this area, however, acknowledge that decisions about GenAI use are locally bound and foreground specific institutional needs.

Rather than focus on the exclusion of GenAI tools from academic settings, a more productive approach is to find thoughtful ways they can be used by students, while simultaneously training faculty to integrate GenAI tools into their pedagogy. This proactive approach will ensure that GenAI's integration aligns with educational values rather than undermining them. This approach, moreover, is neither one of AI-zealotry nor AI-alarmism. It is a middle ground that sees GenAI technologies as tools. The pivot toward tool use thus enables stakeholders to develop proper use-cases that ensure students' authentic engagement with academic topics.

This approach is already occurring in a patchwork manner, with many research-active institutions providing both guidance and encouragement to incorporate GenAI into courses; however, such guidance tends to focus on writing versus STEM subjects (McDonald et al., 2025). Other approaches have opted to reconsider the entire approach to assessment, questioning what it might mean for student work to be "original." Luo (2024), for example, suggests that knowledge production has become a distributed process, necessitating a new way to think about students' original work. More extreme positions even suggest that writing in general will become a "collaborative" process defined by human-AI hybrid approaches that make it difficult to establish originality (Eaton, 2023).

Unfortunately, the oscillation between unsanctioned (or unguided) student use and responses to that use has driven much of the early research on GenAI's effects on students. Much of this work, for example, has examined how GenAI tools affect students' cognition, their academic help-seeking practices (e.g., Macias & Aguilar, 2026), their motivation (Yilmaz & Yilmaz, 2023), and countless other processes that we know matter when it comes to student learning. On the negative side, there have also been many studies that focus on patterns of illicit use (e.g., Cotton et al., 2024), and work that shows students' use of GenAI precludes them from shifting into independent problem solving (e.g., Hak et al., 2025). Such work looks to understand how GenAI affects the *process* of learning in post-secondary settings.

Since GenAI is influencing how universities operate, both through proactive adoption and critical resistance, it is important to take a pragmatic approach and note that not all GenAI use undermines student learning objectives. Work by the USC Center for AI and Society, for example, has incorporated a co-design philosophy (e.g., Steen, 2013) to develop tools that help students process their writing without also giving them the ability to copy and paste the output (Xing & Aguilar, 2026).

Such tools were developed in coordination with writing center faculty to ensure fidelity to learning objectives (e.g., ensuring that students know how to write persuasive arguments that marshal evidence to make claims). Co-design approaches are likely to be fruitful, as they acknowledge that GenAI use is largely unavoidable and thus seeks to develop tools in collaboration with educators responsible for students' academic engagement. Projects like this are cause for hope, as they demonstrate that GenAI tool use is not pre-destined to undermine students' metacognition or critical thinking. Work in this area has also sought student feedback (e.g., Prasad et al., 2025; Zheng et al., 2024), as students will ultimately benefit or suffer from institutional and course-level policies that outline appropriate GenAI use.

Student Concerns About GenAI

It is important to emphasize students' place in the GenAI debate. Those of us on the other side of formal education are already established, yet we often lament the opportunities that students may miss out on with GenAI tools permeating educational institutions. We worry about cognitive laziness, the loss of critical thinking, and other events that might lead to an impoverished learning experience.

Yet, it is clear that students themselves are also concerned about the effects of GenAI on their educational experiences. Their concerns, moreover, often parallel those of faculty, administrators, and professionals. Students worry about becoming too reliant on GenAI and losing the ability to develop deep expertise. English Language Learners, for example, have been shown to be concerned about GenAI over-reliance affecting their ability to learn English (Nelson et al., 2025).

Different attitudes about GenAI also vary based on student populations, with first-year students showing more concern with societal implications of GenAI use when compared to both their older peers and first-generation college students. This work further demonstrates that more senior students and first-generation college students are more concerned about GenAI's impact on their future employment (Tang et al., 2025). Overall, students' evaluation of GenAI's impact is uneven and can vary based on their institutional contexts. National work by Fields and Liu (2025), suggests that students from Massachusetts showed significant concern about "trust in AI performance," whereas students in California rated "accessibility of AI" higher. Given the evolving nature of how GenAI is developed and deployed, however, it would be best to treat such patterns as ephemeral, as they are predicated on evolving policy contexts.

Students' likelihood of using GenAI varies and can be influenced by their familiarity with it. Students with higher AI literacy, for example, are more likely to use it when compared to students with less AI literacy, with the latter group reporting caution and fear (Beckman et al., 2025). When students do use GenAI, they often use it for different reasons, with some opting to use it to achieve quick answers, while others use it as a source of help akin to asking a teaching assistant (Macias & Aguilar, 2026). Students also use GenAI for ideation, brainstorming, and other processes distinct from final written work (Dai, 2025). Other uses have ranged from information retrieval to text paraphrasing (Yusuf et al., 2024)

Some students generally feel comfortable with GenAI use as a means to increase their own productivity (Maxwell et al., 2025), and students' willingness to engage with GenAI predicts their evaluations of GenAI's usefulness—but they can be overconfident with regard to generated content's accuracy (Fayaza et al., 2025). International work shows similar trends, that is, GenAI familiarity predicts use, but demographic differences also appear, for example, men using it more often than women (e.g., Cho & Ofosu-Anim, 2025).

While it is tempting to paint with broad strokes with respect to students' use of GenAI in post-secondary settings, the fact of the matter is that such patterns are dynamic and yet to be established. This is unsurprising; using the concepts I outlined in Chapter 3 and Chapter 4, we can see that all differences in GenAI tool use are attributable to differences in the tools themselves as well as the local sociotechnical systems where students find themselves.

Many differences are thus attributable to what the tools can accomplish. There is no such thing as a "unified" GenAI technology, as such, students all have access to different GenAI tools and have different comfort and competence with respect to using them. Student use of GenAI, moreover, happens within specific institutional—and classroom—contexts that support, undermine, or antagonize the use of a given GenAI tool.

This is why it is difficult to establish broad patterns. Sometimes students use GenAI with formal guidance, other times without. Each pattern of use has different consequences (e.g., Xiu & Aguilar, 2026). In short, students are no different than faculty—each community is dealing with shifting sands that complicate the process of learning. The difference between students and faculty, however, is that it is the latter group's professional responsibility to adapt to the changing landscape so they can prepare their students to do the same.

AI, Employment, and the Future of Human Expertise

Post-secondary education is one of the main pathways to developing expertise. It is a time of focused study and specialization that (hypothetically) leads to more professional opportunities for students. Overall, earning a post-secondary degree has been shown to be a net positive. After analyzing data from over 5.8 million high school and college graduates over the last twenty years, for example, Zhang et al. (2024) found that college is still a good investment, with mean and median internal rates of return (IRR) of over 9 percent.

Importantly, however, rates of return vary as a function of major. They can range from under 5–8 percent for men and women who major in education, the humanities, or the arts, to over 13 percent for engineering majors. This difference in returns is consistent across studies (e.g., Bleemer et al., 2022). Despite such differences, post-secondary degree attainment helps most students, even students who delay graduation while working full time (Witteveen & Attewell, 2021). Further, returns on associate degrees have been shown to be robust over time as well (Minaya et al., 2022).

The introduction to GenAI across sectors, however, has been a disruptive force with regard to both training and employment. Large consulting firms like McKinsey & Company, for example, are building GenAI agents that can do much of the work of first-year analysts (Cutter, 2025). Large tech companies like Microsoft have also mandated the use of AI (Marr, 2025) and have steadily laid off more of their workforce (Halverson, 2025).

The impact of GenAI on employment outcomes is an active area of study. Rafizadeh (2025) for example, has analyzed Bureau of Labor Statistics data spanning December 2000 through April 2025. Findings suggest that there have been "immediate displacement effects (layoff rates increase by 38–101%), coordination failures (quit rates decline by 7–31%, job opening rates fall by 2–45%), and delayed job creation (hiring gains of 1–23% emerge after 12–18 months)." While such impacts are likely attributable tof many forces, GenAI is clearly among them.

There are many examples of disruption across sectors. Tomlinson et al. (2025), for example, found that jobs GenAI might displace range from interpreters to writers to CNC tool programmers to telemarketers, among others (Tomlinson et al., 2025). Thus, it is clear that GenAI is affecting labor and the opportunities students have once they graduate. This includes jobs once seen as harder to automate, including those in sectors such as finance (Joshi, 2025a, 2025b).

The shifting sands of the job market lead to many implications for how students are trained, and how they develop specialized knowledge. We know, for example, that expertise is a function of conducting high-value, non-routine work and having access to opportunities to do so (Kuhlmann & Ardichvili, 2015; National Academies, 2018). Yet, there is a wide variance in how GenAI tools are used in the workplace. Some industries (e.g., software engineering) use GenAI models that are more technical and fine-tuned, whereas others (e.g., content creation) often use off the shelf models (Johri et al., 2025).

The variability in the GenAI tools entry-level professionals use has created further anxieties with regard to what post-secondary training is necessary for students. Unfortunately, knowing what to "train for" is a moving target and sector-dependent, as there is evidence of both displacement (e.g., robotics) and integration focused on improving efficiency (e.g., healthcare) (Salari et al., 2025). In fields such as marketing, there have been calls to balance traditional theories with the need to incorporate knowledge of GenAI tools (Mehmet et al., 2025). As industries move toward automating repetitive tasks and shift toward higher-order tasks, those entering the job market are seeking ways to distinguish their contributions (Mayer et al., 2025).

The good news is that we are far from completely replacing human labor, even in entry-level positions. A pattern across studies is diversity in what training is needed as well as the day-to-day processes that change because of GenAI. It is seldom the case that entire jobs can be done solely by GenAI. Instead, parts of job tasks can be offloaded with supervision.

Student reactions to the perceived changes in jobs due to GenAI disruption are diverse. Along with the potential for job displacement, students in creative fields have been shown to be concerned with maintaining a sense of originality and protecting their intellectual property, rather than being replaced (Shen et al., 2025). Many individuals also grapple with their relationship to GenAI tool use. There is evidence that indicates a tension defined by showing public support for GenAI tools, despite also having internal anxiety about how its deployment might cause job displacement (e.g., Artz & Ren, 2025).

In short, GenAI *is* having an effect on outcomes across sectors, and recent college graduates are very susceptible to the negative effects of chaotic markets. This has compounded anxieties within post-secondary institutions. On the one hand, universities are tasked with educating students in ways that enable them to enter the workforce with a set of marketable skills. On the other hand, much of this training requires the use—or development—of tools that will decrease the number of entry-level jobs. Thus, students are caught in the unenviable position of needing to learn tools that may replace them. This leads to a common dual approach to GenAI: adoption and resistance.

As GenAI tools shape higher education, it is important to take a pragmatic stance, but one that is informed by institutional and individual values. Shifting pedagogical approaches to the whims of the market is a sure way to always be one step behind. Thus, as GenAI continues to infiltrate educational and professional spaces, approaches should focus on core skill development that is nimble. This includes developing critical thinking, so that institutions can mitigate the risk that human expertise will be devalued.

Adoption and Resistance

Tim Marsh, a mentor who has helped me become a better miniature painter, said it best: "kids are asking tools like ChatGPT questions that they should be asking of their parents, friends, and teachers." Why should anyone ask a GenAI tool about creative or personal matters when it has limited visibility into one's life and no real stake in the outcome? Surely, it is better to ask a fellow human being, ideally one with a vested interest in one's success. Thus, deciding *when* to use a GenAI tool is now an important decision with implications that cascade well beyond the initial decision point of using it.

The decision of when to use GenAI is a complex one, and there are many approaches to dealing with the anxieties and excitement of its use in higher education. It is clear that institutions that are nimble and responsive to both the needs of employment markets, as well as the stated needs of their communities, will be positioned well to deal with future changes—or disruptions—as they occur. This requires interrogating the implementation of GenAI at all levels.

My own work in this area focuses on researching GenAI's impact on education while also pushing back against unchecked adoption (e.g., Aguilar et al., 2024). More recent work has centered on co-design philosophy as an important part of this approach. Collaboration and stakeholder involvement are vital, especially when the goal is to thoughtfully integrate GenAI tool use into educational settings (Aguilar et al., 2025; Villatoro et al., 2021; Steen, 2013).

Community input matters. What is clear is that there will be patterns of both adoption and resistance that will vary both between and within institutions. Early work in this area has shown that classroom policies are sometimes clearer when compared to institutional policies, which leads to fragmented student experiences (Jiang et al., 2025; Giles et al., 2025). Further, this variability can lead to disciplinary bias, that is, scientific disciplines with more GenAI exposure and use are developing more nuanced frameworks of adoption, when compared to disciplines that remain avoidant of GenAI (Wang et al., 2025). Internal reports from AI companies have also indicated that divergence in use is common among students, with STEM students using tools like Anthropic's Claude more often when compared to students in the humanities (Anthropic Education Report, 2025).

Reasons for adopting GenAI will be varied, but may include convenience. Some students, for example, may feel more comfortable communicating with GenAI chatbots because it enables them to avoid attending to formalities or etiquette (e.g., Shin et al., 2024). Trust in GenAI tools is an important factor, as the more a GenAI tool is trusted, the more likely it will be used (Wang, Li, et al., 2025). GenAI use is not always problematic, however, as it can support students' intrinsic motivation by supporting autonomy (e.g., Li et al., 2025b).

It is clear that GenAI tool use will affect many sectors, which creates an imperative to address it in all domains. We would do well to remember that learning is defined by overcoming both discomfort and failures in order to master concepts, so it is important to give students opportunities to struggle. When GenAI tools eliminate such struggles we should be wary of GenAI tool use.

This leads us back to where we started: local decisions will be paramount to success in a world where GenAI tools are ubiquitous. However, such decisions should attend to external factors (e.g., job markets) so that they are made in a way that supports student mastery over the emerging GenAI tools that are poised to shape many sectors. This, however, does not mean overextending to tool use; instead, approaches to adoption and resistance should move beyond tools and toward reinforcing critical thinking.

9

The Future of Education with GenAI

Chapter Outline

Introduction

Academics are averse to speculation, and rightly so. Our profession demands that all of the claims we make in writing be warranted by the evidence available at the moment. This can create a tension, however, because the academic publication cycle is often slower than we'd like it to be. "Hurry up and publish that so I can cite it," is a sentence I've uttered at least a few times.

Good science—rigorous science—is necessarily slow, and I respect the slower pace. The tortoise did win the race against the hare, after all. If we take a long-term view of things, that fable gives us comfort. Thus, while I don't know if the arc of history actually bends toward justice, I *do* know that as long as we follow the scientific method, the arc of history will bend toward progress and technological advancement.

Still, the current moment suggests that the slow and steady approach, while good for science in general, leaves many of us sidelined when it comes to shaping the public discourse about areas we know a lot about. To compound matters, we also live in the age of ubiquitous misinformation, one where "influencers" command large audiences that shape the public discourse in ways that can be both problematic and *utterly* incorrect. This can be frustrating, since we academics know more than our slow publication cycle demonstrates. Yet, many of us are trained to not engage with the broader discourse—even if it intersects with our expertise.

This chapter sits at the boundary of speculation. Up to this point, I have been a (mostly) traditional academic. Consequently, my claims followed the model you might expect. Claims grounded by the evidence at hand. This should hopefully help those who wish to better understand GenAI's impact on education make evidence-based decisions when faced with integrating GenAI tools into their instructional contexts, be they classrooms, homes, or offices.

I now give myself permission to speculate based on what I suspect will happen in the years to come. Why? Because I find that academics are uniquely positioned to *guess* (or to hypothesize, if you want to be technical about it), regarding what might come next when discussing our areas of expertise. That is what this concluding chapter is about.

I have been in the field of educational technology for long enough to see patterns emerge. History does not repeat itself exactly, but events have a way of following a similar cadence if one pays enough attention. So, while GenAI in education will not follow the same exact patterns I've seen before, I am confident that we will see permutations of those patterns. The final pages of this book, then, are speculative—albeit the educated kind. I should note that I am perfectly fine with being 100 percent incorrect in my speculation, though I suspect that I won't be.

Future Decision Points

Educators and their institutions have to decide if, when, and how GenAI will be a part of their daily lives. These decisions, moreover, are not always up to educators. Students will act in accordance with the pressures that they face both within and outside of school. GenAI tool use represents an interesting course of action, as there are blurry boundaries between what counts as cheating and what doesn't. This puts both students and educators at a crossroads, one where they have to decide their level of engagement and what sort of training they'll need to make the most use of GenAI without falling into the trap of overusing it.

The goal of this book has been to give teachers, students, parents, and policymakers a framework for thinking about GenAI. It would be hopeless to provide a "guide" that tells each stakeholder group how to use a given tool. The field is developing too quickly and there are too many competing interests that will shape what counts as proper/improper use of GenAI. Instead, my goal has been to provide a series of frameworks drawn from psychology, philosophy, design, and ethics to ground any discussion about GenAI, so that all of the stakeholders involved in the decisions around GenAI use can have common ground. It is my hope that this framework will empower individuals to interrogate their use of GenAI—no matter how limited that use happens to be.

This is what I mean by *Authenticating Intelligence*. In the end, all of the aforementioned stakeholder groups will be in the position to determine "what counts" in their respective contexts. They will, in a very real sense, be the authenticat*ors* of intelligence. This is not a new process, but it feels different because human language was, up until a few decades ago, the sole domain of humans. This is no longer the case, so it is the responsibility of everyone involved to determine what counts as human intelligence as applied to a particular task, and what doesn't. Distinguishing the synthetic and the authentic is now paramount.

Such distinctions are particularly important to educators who are the arbiters of what counts in their classrooms. They will decide if students use GenAI tools in their classrooms, and how such uses are contextualized. It is my hope that they make those decisions based on sound science, transparent values, and a sense of agency over the process. They should not, in my view, be subjected to the whims of a tech industry that is incentivized to overpromise in order to maximize market share and the value of their products.

Up to this point, I have argued that while GenAI will be integrated into educational systems, it will not bring about the sweeping transformation many anticipate. Instead, generative AI tools will quickly become mundane. That does not mean that GenAI will not have an *impact* (it will), but just as smartphones have been relegated to the common, so too will GenAI become common, its effects present, but not always salient.

In the remaining pages of this book I speculate over potential decision points of stakeholders, and game out the ramifications of such decisions. My speculation is grounded in all of my training and experiences, and as such will ring true for many. However, I am not a fortune teller; in fact, as I have shown, predictions have a way of being gloriously incorrect, and I suspect many of mine will be. Thus, you should treat the remaining pages as food for thought, so that you can create meaningful thought experiments of your own as you read through how I navigate mine.

(De)Regulation and Disruption

As I write this section, much of the disruption that is affecting education in the United States is being caused by the US government. I do not know if this disruption will become permanent and reshape what education looks like in the United States in the decades to come, but what I do know is that this sort of disruption is exactly the sort of environment where EdTech thrives.

This is partially because with imposed austerity there can be a misguided and myopic fetishization of efficiency. Elon Musk's DOGE, for example, was a spectacular failure in finding efficiencies in our government (e.g., Demirjian & Nehamas, 2025). Yet, I do not expect the lesson was learned. Formal education in the United States may suffer from similar "bull in the China shop" approaches to "innovation" and "efficiency."

While a tautology, it is essential to remember that disrup*tion* is disrup*tive*. The role of a disrupter is to seek and find a system that is working fine, but "inefficiently." Once found, the system can be broken, examined, and rebuilt. In this dynamic, two things emerge: a new system that is potentially more innovative (but sometimes only *differently* innovative), and a new set of masters who run it.

Uber displaced taxis and made third-party transportation easier for the end user, but there is nothing terribly important about seeing an image of a car draw closer to me before I get into the car. Has it been a net good? Perhaps, but not without real costs and a number of broken laws (Collier et al., 2018). It is not an overstatement to say that what is left after "disruption" is not only a broken system to be rebuilt, but a series of broken people who would have otherwise lived happily with the status quo.

To the disruptor, this reality is distasteful—the antithesis to progress. To the person being disrupted, this reality is their *life*. One that perhaps should not have been upended to fulfill the ambitions of those who seek to enrich themselves using the new system they've put in place over the one they tore down.

In typical times we might turn to the process of government regulation to ensure that the disruptor is not given *carte blanche* to remake a system that serves private interests at the expense of public goods. This will likely not be the case when considering how GenAI is deployed within our schools. GenAI's ingress into different educational environments and institutions will occur in a friendly regulatory environment, given that in 2025 the Trump administration signed an executive order effectively deregulating AI (The White House, 2025b). Such a move is incorrect, though it is useful to explore why I make that assertion.

Much like the rest of this book, my position is nuanced and asks us to examine both the affordances and limitations of government regulation, and what a deregulated environment might yield versus one that supports some regulations developed in good faith. Such an approach would ensure that GenAI development and deployment isn't simply an extension of the collective goals of large tech companies.

I do not presume to know what all of those goals are, but by definition, such goals must be motivated by profit and capturing market share. Otherwise, the interests of shareholders would be ignored. Thus, the limited set of goals that tech companies have is not always aligned with the goals of the student, the teacher, the administrator, or the parent. Educators care about how children and adults learn and are typically less concerned with which company makes money doing it. We would do well to interrogate the motivations of those who would wish to operate without oversight—or with freedom to completely ignore such oversight.

Yet, my argument isn't grounded in the idea that we should be heavy-handed with regulation. I am a firm believer in the potential of market-driven innovation, as private enterprise has a way of being nimble and responsive to the needs that government might be slower to address. Unfortunately, private enterprise also has a habit of manufacturing needs that would not exist without its intervention. Thus, my position vis-à-vis regulation is nuanced; I believe that regulation is a mechanism to think beyond the market and foreground the needs of communities, especially those that might not have the economic power to exercise any influence. This is particularly important as we consider how GenAI will be integrated into schools and universities.

We saw this clearly during the pandemic. Communities historically ignored by broadband providers struggled to have high-speed internet that would have enabled them to participate more fully in remote instruction (Aguilar et al., 2022; Ferguson, 2004). Regulation is a way to ensure that there are multiple voices included when thinking about how GenAI will be integrated into our educational institutions.

Such a process would ideally include the voice of experts, end users, and everyone who might benefit or suffer from the use of GenAI tools within educational spaces. Yes, this process is *necessarily* slower than a pure market-driven approach. That is fine in my view, as we are not a collection of dollars to be spent on the products provided. We are human beings living in communities that should have pathways to exercise our collective autonomy—even if that autonomy pushes against what some might call "innovation."

Given current trends, however, it is unlikely that regulation will occur, so I posit that when GenAI is deployed in different educational environments it will be done with limited evidence regarding its efficacy. The field of education will then concern itself with post-mortem investigations over how different approaches worked better than others. Many will find that GenAI tools failed spectacularly in certain contexts.

EdTech has been in this position before (Chapter 3), so I do not see GenAI providing a different set of answers to the same questions. Instead, I suspect that (as with all innovation), those with more resources will benefit the most while simultaneously having more agency over what happens. Those with fewer resources, however, will be subjected to poorly thought-out plans that will waste money (at best) and harm students' learning trajectories (at worst). In short, we can prevent the negative consequences of GenAI use in schools, but will almost certainly choose not to.

Snake Oil 2.0

It would be naive to assume that GenAI will not be disruptive, as I have shown that it has already shifted many approaches within educational institutions. Ultimately, I am weary of disruption, but it is unavoidable and will continue as GenAI tools become more ubiquitous. As I have argued in the preceding chapters, GenAI tools are well positioned to change the ways students learn and teachers teach. I have also argued that the changes happening now are not necessarily miracles in innovation, and are instead governed by a set of affordances and limitations (Chapter 4). GenAI is capable of many things, and it is also unable to do many things.

Proper use of GenAI-powered tools, then, requires students, educators, and administrators to ethically leverage what GenAI can do, while avoiding overextending its usefulness beyond its capabilities. This is necessary for educators to keep in mind as they are solicited by EdTech companies. Unless those who control the purse strings of their institutions are diligent, they might succumb to fast-talking EdTech salesmen who are incentivized to overpromise. In the years to come, we should all be wary of *GenAI Snake Oil 2.0.*

Looking back, over 100 years ago *Clark Stanley's Snake Oil Liniment* was sold as a panacea (Friedman, 2024). Suffering from arthritis? A sore throat? Hay fever? Snake Oil Liniment was your answer. As you might expect, it turns out that *Clark Stanley's Snake Oil Liniment* was actually mineral oil and trace amounts of other chemicals. Unsurprisingly, Snake Oil was found to be drastically overpriced and of limited value, and has become our go-to term for fraudulent products that, at best, drastically underdeliver. We also associate unscrupulous salesmen with the product, as we assume such salesmen were aware they were selling something bogus.

When we consider the claims made about GenAI and education, I cannot help but assume that are are in the throes of Snake Oil 2.0—or, as an EdTech investor near you will call it "generative AI solutions to education." One of the first high-profile cases for this type of fraud was perpetuated by Joanna Smith-Griffin, whose company was contracted by the Los Angeles Unified School District (LAUSD).

Smith-Griffin was indicted on counts of fraud and associated financial crimes (Blume, 2024). She and her accomplices defrauded both investors and the families who were hoping for a technology that could help their children learn. Smith-Griffin is, I fear, the first in what is likely a long line of EdTech hucksters who will travel school-to-school selling their claims that GenAI can do things it cannot. Such hucksters will not be in the majority, but they don't need to be in order to do lasting damage. In a deregulated AI environment, the line between Snake Oil and real product may even appear blurry.

Unlike the snake oil of old, GenAI snake oil is insidious because it is enveloped in a thin veneer of techno-babble that is intertwined with actually useful applications. This strategy of mixing useful applications with fantastic promises is intended to take advantage of people who see GenAI doing interesting things, but incorrectly assume that a few generated parlor tricks can replace authentic learning experiences for students.

I hold that this pattern of overpromising while underdelivering is especially dangerous for organizations, like school districts, that are chronically underfunded and on the lookout for ways to become more efficient, while giving students what they sorely need: personal attention. Rather than investing in the profession of teaching, however, venture capitalists are flocking to finance startups that align with useful applications (e.g., $118 billion raised in 2025; Teare, 2025). Yet, some are also helping to develop GenAI Snake Oil 2.0. I do not see this interest abating in the years to come.

Investors are allowed to do whatever they like with their money so long as it is legal. We as consumers and educators, however, have a responsibility to question the claims of EdTech startups. We must further examine the implications of putting technology in front of our children. Thus, a mitigation against being sold GenAI Snake Oil is to ask for scientifically vetted findings, not technobabble and PowerPoint presentations that are little more than "AI + YOU = LEARNING."

Educators would do well to question "freemium" models as applied to GenAI EdTech offerings. What starts as cost-effective innovation, or "freemium models," often results in the fragmentation of cost and value. An example is helpful here. When Uber first started, there was no such thing as "Uber Black"—there was simply Uber. But as the technology matured, there were more varied experiences riders could have. Do you want to ride in a black car? Well, then, simply pay more and you can ride in a car that is black, or one that will actually come get you where you are, as opposed to having to walk some distance to a pickup spot. (I'm looking at you, LAX International Airport.)

This sort of diversity in offerings is perfectly fine, and generally unproblematic when we are discussing something as simple as entering and exiting a vehicle that takes one from point A to point B. However, this sort of diversification becomes problematic when we apply it to education. It is no surprise that students have different experiences with our educational system based on income.

However, up until recently we saw those differences, those "inequities," as something to fight against. We aimed to find mitigations to lessen the gaps, provide more opportunities, and generally try to make sure everyone had access to a good education. This attitude seems to be waning, and I fear that GenAI applications in education will normalize the idea that it is okay for students to have access to different GenAI-powered experiences based on income band.

I suspect that this reality is unavoidable and assume that students in low-income public schools will be able to use "free" GenAI models that are less sophisticated, more likely to hallucinate, and potentially more biased in problematic ways. After all, "better" models will cost money. All the while, I suspect that students who use these impoverished versions of GenAI tools will also train the next generation of GenAI technologies. This has always been the trade-off in tech: use a product for free or nearly free while tacitly (or explicitly) granting permission for your data and behaviors to be captured and used to evolve the technology.

This is not necessarily a bad trade; I am fine with Google Maps knowing where I am going since that knowledge is necessary to help get me there. There is added complexity, however, when it comes to using data from students. When I get lost on the road, it does not (usually) alter my life trajectory. When students get lost learning new material, though, there may very well be developmental consequences.

I have a general distaste for the fact that the current tech ecosystem is focused on disrupting for the sake of innovation, that is, breaking what is established in hopes that the disarray caused can lead to new products that capture market share. I anticipate this model will be used in GenAI and education. All of that said, I am an optimist! I am a firm believer in the positive impacts of GenAI's integration into education, but I fear that we are in too much of a rush to realize gains without understanding the true costs.

In an effort to innovate, we often cast aside our better judgment—or simply our slower judgment—in hopes that we can operate along the cutting edge of technology. Unfortunately, cutting edges are sharp and indifferent to whom they harm. There's a reason Silicon Valley's motto has been "move fast and break things." Our children's education, however, should not be on the list of "breakables."

When it comes to the education of our children, and the organizations tasked with providing that education, it is important to encourage tempered judgment on the part of our education leaders. Joanna Smith-Griffin won't be the first person charged with selling AI snake oil, but hopefully, we can all learn from her example and not assume that AI is the panacea for all of our educational worries.

Resistance and Acceptance Among Educators

This book began with the thesis that GenAI will not "revolutionize" education. Instead, GenAI tools will become mundane parts of our lives. It is my hope that I have convinced you of this possibility. In education, the new reality with respect to GenAI integration will be the product of some resistance coupled with experimentation. In both K12 spaces and post-secondary spaces, GenAI integration will hinge on the values of educators (and those enabled or endorsed by their institutions) vis-à-vis education, rather than GenAI tools themselves.

I am the first to admit that EdTech writ large has been a positive force in the lives of educators and students. Advances such as learning management systems, cloud-based documents, and student information systems have nudged education in positive ways by helping reduce administrative burdens (e.g., Frazier & Hearrington, 2024). More recent technologies like cognitive tutors and learning analytics have also helped move us closer to understanding student behaviors (Baker et al., 2004;

Borchers et al., 2024), and personalizing instruction for students (Baker, 2016; Roberts et al., 2017).

Despite the gains brought on by different EdTech products, I begin this section with a potentially controversial assertion: educators are correct to be skeptical about GenAI tools, and AI more broadly. Skepticism is healthy and necessary, as it enables us to understand the boundary conditions of educational technologies, so that we can better know when to deploy them, and when to avoid them in lieu of "tried and true" methods.

Educator skepticism in the current "AI moment," moreover, is informed by the philosophy of disruption in the tech field, that is, move fast, break things, and capture the market share once you've put things back together. Often, this emerging market leaves behind those who would have shaped its evolution (e.g., cab drivers vs. Uber). What does education look like without educators? This is a question that both the tech industry and educators themselves are asking, with differing views of the world that would emerge.

Yet, not all educators have the same set of concerns, hopes, or imperatives. Educators, be they K12 teachers or university faculty, have varied responses to what it means to use GenAI in their profession and in their classrooms. The effects of GenAI on each of their professions will also vary, as they each have unique sets of imperatives that inform the pedagogical choices they make. That is why I see two potential futures for educators. I discuss each in turn.

For K12 teachers, GenAI in education will define their profession in ways that are intertwined with where they happen to teach. That is because education in the United States is a decentralized, locally controlled endeavor (Polikoff, 2021). This fact leads to differing experiences among educators and students. Still, I suspect that we are likely to see broad patterns across contexts. GenAI tools, for example, will continue to evolve such that they will likely become tools that K12 educators can "pilot" much like we pilot/drive our vehicles. If we run with that analogy, we see that in order to pilot a vehicle one must understand its affordances and its limitations.

GenAI tools also need to be active in an environment that supports their use. With those pieces in place, the relationship between teacher and GenAI tool will become a cooperative one. The level of cooperation, however, will obviously differ based on experience, resources, and comfort with GenAI. In the best-case scenario, GenAI tools will become mundane and unnoticed over time. K12 teachers will simply *use* GenAI in their jobs when and where it is necessary, and also deal with limitations as they arise. In this world, GenAI will give K12 teachers more cognitive freedom to act in ways that benefit their students. I predict that this world will be the most likely one to emerge once GenAI hype has died down.

That does not mean that teaching *as a profession* won't be impacted. It will. Even before GenAI disruption, teaching as a profession was already on the decline. More shocks to the profession due to GenAI may accelerate declines, but the teachers that remain will have more tools at their disposal. This does not mean that they will, however, be better compensated or more respected for their work. Thus, in the years to come GenAI will not emerge as a tool that completely replaces K12 educators. Instead educators will have access to a constellation of tools that make their professional lives easier—to a point.

Post-secondary educators, that is, faculty who teach at vocational schools, universities, and community colleges, will face different sets of challenges than K12 educators. This is because post-secondary educators operate from a differing set of imperatives and serve different types of students. Often, one sees post-secondary educators as teaching a group of 18- to 22-year-olds fresh out of high school, but that is not a realistic picture of what higher education looks like anymore. Instead, faculty teach older students, as well as graduate students—including PhD students. What all post-secondary educators have in common is that they teach adults, and adult students have adult challenges and capabilities.

This is why, in the years to come, I suspect that concerns about academic integrity will remain at the forefront of many faculty, and for good reason. As students continue to introduce GenAI into their workflows, there have been concerns raised over the effects it has regarding their ability to do independent work in the future (Macias & Aguilar, 2026; Maxwell et al., 2025). At the time of this book's writing (circa 2025), there have been differing responses to students' use of GenAI. Each response, be it a ban or full integration into the curricula, stems from both the instructor's comfort with GenAI, as well as the field's response to the technology.

Much like K12 education in the United States is decentralized, so too is post-secondary education. So much so, in fact, that I would argue that institutional policies will remain open to faculty interpretation, as to not stymie potential innovation while respecting instructor autonomy. This general policy of "we will not police GenAI use so long as academic integrity remains intact," will necessarily have different interpretations among faculty, not least because faculty often have competing responsibilities that include research and service, on top of teaching.

How GenAI technologies affect faculty will vary by institution type, rank, and attitudes of their specific fields. Computer scientists, for example, will need to grapple with phenomena such as "vibe coding" (Ray, 2025; Meske et al., 2025), while those in the humanities will do what they can to preserve students' critical thinking vis-à-vis writing (Qadir et al., 2024; Helal et al., 2025).

Regardless of who the educator serves, however, there is cause to be wary of overreliance on GenAI in educational spaces. A potential consequence of overusing GenAI will be a decline in deep subject expertise as educators become increasingly reliant on GenAI tools to be more productive. While this will not affect the expertise of educators within well-resourced regions, over time, true specialists may become rarer, with many educators in under-resourced schools relegated to become mere operators of GenAI tools.

The Rise of GenAI Tutors

Up until now I've speculated broadly and discussed potential trends in policy and practice. What about *actual* technologies that will be in front of students and teachers? How might we anticipate what is coming so that we can evaluate it better and make good decisions? In order to look forward, it's worth looking backward a bit. *Generative* AI may be new, but AIED (AI and Education) isn't and has been creating many technologies for decades that help students of all ages learn. There have been recent calls within the field, in fact, to ensure that GenAI does not overshadow the need to have an asset-based approach to instruction and assessment using GenAI (e.g., Ocumpaugh et al., 2024).

This is partially why I began referring to GenAI technologies as either *Synthetic Human Language Machines* (SHLMs) or *Synthetic Human Artifact Machines* (SHAMs). Language is powerful, and this distinction forces the reader (you) to interact with GenAI as a machine, as opposed to a person. Machines have affordances, limitations, and we do not treat them as though they need special attention or care when we address them.

Human beings also have limitations, but we generally do not refer to human beings as "having affordances," as most of us (correctly) bristle at merely seeing our fellow humans as tools and commodities.

Before SHLMs or SHAMs, there were cognitive tutors. Many focused on math instruction, such as Carnegie Learning's Cognitive Tutor (Corbett et al., 2001), or ASSISTments (Heffernan & Heffernan, 2014). Tools like these were powerful because they enabled personalization through detecting patterns in students' misunderstandings, providing hints to help them move forward, and generally serve as good scaffolds that enabled students to stay engaged. The results of these technologies are well documented and have led to positive benefits.

The difference between cognitive tutors and GenAI tools of today, however, is that they do not mimic human interaction in the same way. Human language is programmed in cognitive tutors, but it is not *generated* through the use of LLMs. . This leads to a more limited experience—it is unlikely that students who used cognitive tutors ever perceived them as having real agency or being "human-like." This is also a key affordance of the technology; students see cognitive tutors as tools that help them master concepts in math, not a friend. It also gave teachers insights into misunderstandings.

All of this is set to change with the proliferation of GenAI-based tutoring systems that can do what traditional cognitive tutors did, but with the added responsiveness of chat interfaces. There are already such systems in place, and many more are being developed by companies like *Magic School* (Magic School, Inc., n.d.). These GenAI systems are set to potentially change classrooms and instructional practices across K12 and post-secondary institutions.

Yet, as GenAI tutors become increasingly available to students, I suspect that the quality of these tools will vary significantly, with only select groups gaining access to the best systems. This is the nature of all technology, including educational technology; those with more resources get systems with better safeguards, more computational power, and so on. Students from disadvantaged backgrounds will get systems that are fine, but limited. Many will not be personalized to the same degree, leading to unequal experiences, and potentially interactions that lead to unequal outcomes.

This is why I am always wary of those who point to the potential for GenAI tutors to help disadvantaged students. When uneven access is the norm, it seems likely that uneven access to the latest GenAI innovations will persist. Thus, those on the wrong side of the digital divide will remain there in the era of GenAI tutors. This is inevitable, as we have not done the work to fix systemic issues that cause digital divides to begin with.

A Teacher's Roles in the Age of AI

Here I present at least two possibilities for teachers. In all likelihood, there will be groups of teachers who are subjected to each reality, and many who will oscillate between them as GenAI continues to make inroads into schools. First, the positive view.

As I have discussed, GenAI is a powerful technology because it has the potential to personalize the synthetic content it generates based on data it ingests. This data starts with what one might consider "vanilla" models, or models that were not *purposefully* biased to serve a particular purpose. Starting with this basis, models can be modified to suit a particular task. In this positive speculation about how this will happen for teachers, I suspect that there will come a time in the near future where teachers can personalize the content they teach in a way that is more granular.

When I was a middle school teacher, for example, I had thirty students and what felt like five reading levels. What that meant in practice was dealing with the "Goldilocks" problem. Some students received content that was above their reading ability, many received content that was appropriate, and still others were bored because the content was not challenging. This was true across domains, and also varied *within* students. I had an English language learner, for example, who had trouble reading English, but was ahead of the class when it came to math. As you might imagine, such challenges have a way of compounding. Teachers have to decide how they will teach to "the average," and how they will "differentiate" (personalize) content for students on either end of the spectrum.

This is a nearly impossible task, and one that will be alleviated with GenAI tools that can personalize reading difficulty (Hidayat, 2024). Not only can they do that, they can also take students" interests and infuse them into content, so that students can see both themselves and what they're interested in reflected in the content they use to learn (Li et al., 2025). This is an *extraordinarily* powerful tool for teachers, as it makes differentiation a reachable goal, instead of an abstraction that one aims for.

Future teachers will not only be able to differentiate, they will be able to offload more mundane, time-consuming, and generally obnoxious tasks to GenAI agents. Monitored auto grading, for example, will potentially become the norm, as will GenAI-assisted lesson planning. In short, the administrative tasks of teaching may be relegated to GenAI so that the *art* of teaching can become more of a focus. In this world, teachers will have more time to build relationships with students, diagnose particular patterns of learning and difficulty for their students, and do so with a facility that was unimaginable in 2020. In short, there will be reduced friction when it comes to teaching.

I am confident that the above set of circumstances will become the reality for many teachers. Yet, I am equally certain that the following will occur. As GenAI tools become more capable and ubiquitous, there will be increasing arguments that question the role of the teacher as the primary educator. Why bother with low student-teacher ratios, after all, if we can simply park students in front of capable GenAI tools that can accommodate their learning needs quickly and "efficiently"?

Though I do speculate here, I would be remiss to not mention that such models are already being considered and planned for (e.g., Alpha Schools). If we continue down this line of thinking, we can see multiple types of models emerging. Students may, for example, have "GenAI pullout" time, when large groups get together for GenAI-driven instruction, with an adult "monitor" that may or may not have direct teaching experience. We might extend that model further and question low student-teacher ratios altogether and suppose that one teacher could manage a room of fifty students. After all, most of the instruction will be handled by GenAI tools.

Thus, both negative and positive consequences will result from educators' interactions with GenAI. Positive consequences include more time for personal 1:1 instruction, personalized learning resources for students, and more efficient workflows. Yet, as GenAI-driven educational technologies grow in capacity and expertise, there is a risk of further undervaluing educators and the possibility for relaxed standards for who becomes a teacher. It may, for example, be presumed that GenAI will do the heavy lifting. As a result, some educators will become mere operators of GenAI technologies, while others with years of expertise and experience will move to places that still value human interaction.

So we are left with at least two probable worlds. One where educators offload some of their responsibilities to finely tuned GenAI models to help them become better at their jobs. Another where educators are replaced entirely. I imagine both will occur, and that this shift will be uneven, with wealthier schools benefiting the most from cutting-edge systems. Moreover, both of the scenarios I've outlined above will manifest simultaneously and along predictable socioeconomic lines.

Commodification of Expertise

One of the most fascinating developments when it comes to the increasing integration of GenAI into our lived experiences is how we are beginning to cope with non-human ("synthetic") expertise. During the past decade we have witnessed an erosion of what it means to be an expert, up to and including denying science as a basis for making decisions. I will not comment on those developments here, as they are covered well by others (see Sinatra & Hofer, 2021).

Instead, I am interested in the *commodification* of expertise, and how such commodification is and will be enacted through GenAI. What does it mean when expert knowledge is, in a very real sense, divorced from the expert? What role do experts have, if any, when it comes to vetting synthetic information—and what are the safeguards in place to protect non-experts from making decisions based on flawed reasoning, flawed evidence, or GenAI hallucinations?

My discussion of expertise, and its commodification, presupposes the well-supported conclusions of others, as well as my own personal experience as a scholar. Namely, it's hard being an expert these days. In the past, to be an expert was to possess hard-earned knowledge about a topic, or area of study, and to have the authority to speak on those topics.

Experts still have that knowledge, but it does not automatically come with the authority it used to. In fact, the very nature of what it means to *be* "an expert" has been questioned, pushed on, eroded, so that we (the experts) find ourselves in a precarious position where we must explain *why* others should listen to us. There was a time when most tacitly accepted the fact that experts had the authority to comment on topics they spent their entire professional lives studying. Having to marshal evidence in support of what used to be a premise (i.e., listen to me because I, quite literally, know better than you), is exhausting. I do not blame my colleagues for not always "fighting the good fight" in that regard.

Much to the collective dismay of my fellow experts, GenAI has emerged—and it continues to expand—during the same time that many question our ability to *be* experts at all. To state it bluntly: true expertise is seemingly fragile and exists in a world where the ability to create expert-sounding prose has multiplied exponentially.

To compound matters, the use of GenAI makes it difficult (if not impossible) to trace the chain of evidence that grounds an argument back to its original source. Sometimes the results of this process lead to funny developments, like when Google's infant LLM told folks that Elmer's glue could be used to make the cheese on pizza better (Paul, 2024). A through-line of this book has been the idea that GenAI turns expertise into commodities that can be replicated with modest effort. I suspect that the result of this "perfect storm" will be the true commodification of expertise, down to a "tiered" system of what sort of GenAI "expert" one has access to.

What might this look like in higher education? A potential analog is what happens with other tech developments, that is, a tiered system of access that begins with "free" versions and scales to the more expensive, more sophisticated versions. I suspect that access to the highest quality GenAI models will be gated behind paywalls and accessible only to those with sufficient resources. Universities may eventually turn inward and attempt to commodify their faculty's expertise by turning their written work into GenAI resources or chatbots.

Versions of this have already occurred when it comes to content created by faculty during the pandemic for remote learning (e.g., Koenig, 2021). In this case, who owned recorded lectures was debated, and debates were complicated when faculty died. While some educators may resist this shift, many will find themselves accepting the new reality as their roles are diminished by GenAI tools. Some may even see some benefits to having their GenAI personas turned into commodities through something akin to residual payments. Yet, I suspect that the standard salaries of educators will not increase and will instead likely continue to stagnate.

GenAI replications of expertise, I hold, will be impoverished versions of the original, but that does not preclude universities from preserving and commodifying the work of their faculty through GenAI resources. I also imagine that there will be litigation associated with who owns GenAI personas of experts once those experts die. (For what it's worth, if GenAI Replicant Dr. Aguilar ever becomes a thing, I would prefer that my family profit from it.)

In K12 education, similar commodification will occur, though data will be gathered from more vulnerable populations: students. This will likely happen through their use of GenAI tools, which may or may not help them learn (the science is still out on efficacy). Unfortunately, I imagine that there will be insufficient conversations (and zero regulation) when considering the ethical problems with commodifying student insights and struggles within systems that they had no choice but to use. This isn't to say that there won't be pushback. There has been, and there will continue to be. Along with this pushback, best practices will emerge, so it isn't the case that GenAI use will lead to a dystopian future for students.

As students, teachers, administrators, and parents navigate this process, there will be discussions and/or arguments about how such use will yield even more innovation and more personalized instruction. I suspect that many such arguments will be in good faith and may actually yield something useful. I also suspect, however, that students whose cognition is being captured through the use of GenAI models will not profit from it. Whether or not they should is a valid question, and one that should be answered since students' intellectual labor is going to transform the future of GenAI-driven educational products.

Ceding Cognition

Cogito, ergo sum. I think, therefore I am; René Descartes coined this phrase in *Discourse on the Method* (Descartes, 1641). It is beyond the scope of this book, however, to examine Cartesian dualism (i.e., the idea that the mind and the body are two distinct entities). Instead, I invoke Descartes's most famous phrase to remind us that *thinking* is an essential part of what it means to be human. It is also what many tech giants hope to capture and recreate as they move toward AGI models. How long that will take is anyone's guess. Instead of focusing on an uncertain future inhabited by thinking machines, it is better to focus on more proximal issues, focused on how we will use GenAI tools.

If we believe Descartes and hold that cognition—the ability to think—is the seat of the soul, or at least a core part of what it means to be a human being, then we should consider what it means to *cede* some of our cognition to GenAI tools that do not actually think. You may be asking: What do I mean by “cede cognition”? I can illustrate the core idea with a (true) short story.

There was once a vacant seat for Detroit Public Schools Community School District, and the seat was filled through a process where prospective candidates answered a set of questions that were evaluated by serving members of the board. The questions were straightforward, including: “What contributions can you make to the school district,” “Describe how you'll advocate openness and democratic processes in all board activities with emphasis on team decision-making and consensus,” and "From your perspective, what are the challenges facing our school district?”

The phrasing of the last question is essential: *From. Your. Perspective.* It was thus surprising that one of the candidates for this seat responded with the following (Dellinger & Walker, 2025; Detroit Public School Board, 2025):

> **ChatGPT You said**: How should I respond to this question as it pertains to my interest in a vacant DPSCD school board seat: What approach would you take to help pass millage renewals, millage increases or Headlee override elections? **ChatGPT said**: Here's a strong and strategic way to respond to that question, tailored to your candidacy for a vacant DPSCD school board seat: Question: What approach would you take to help pass millage renewals, millage increases, or Headlee override elections? Response: As a proud Detroiter, lifelong educator, and committed advocate for our children and communities, I understand that millage renewals, increases, and Headlee override elections are not just about dollars—they are about ensuring our students have access to safe, high-quality learning environments and the resources they need to thrive.

This mistake makes it clear that the words that the board members evaluated were the unedited “perspective” of ChatGPT, circa 2025. I do not have to linger on why this is problematic. Retelling this story is not meant to elicit *Schadenfreude*. Instead, this candidate's actions illustrate what I mean when I say that, in an era of ubiquitous GenAI, there will be those who choose to cede their cognition over to GenAI tools like ChatGPT.

Unethical use of GenAI tools is not merely problematic because it breaks norms for what we think should count as an authentic contribution. It is problematic because it is indicative of choices that cede one's cognitive capacities in order to masquerade as more competent, or worse, to simply get out of doing the work. The tragedy of stories like the one above is that the potential candidate may very well have been a wonderful member of the school board, one that was focused on doing what's best for students in her district. Yet, by ceding her cognition over to ChatGPT, her contributions will never be felt.

I suspect that such events will become more common, such that they will no longer elicit negative responses. Instead, ceding cognition to GenAI tools will become common enough that language will catch up to such uses. Perhaps a person's ability to "pilot" AI will be seen as a virtue—regardless of the fact that doing so is merely a reduction of one's cognitive capacities.

This reduction, in order to create a deliverable for another entity that has no stake in one's personal or professional development, is the real danger to the future of education. Thus, in the future we may move away from *I think therefore I am* and toward: *I eliminate thought, therefore I am not*, or *Cogitationem elido; ergo non sum*. If this is the path forward, then GenAI will not need to have taken over, for we will have already ceded a core part of what it means to be human to those who would equate synthetic language with human expression.

A Warning

GenAI tools are seductive because they create frictionless interaction experiences (i.e., query leads to answer) that *feel* intelligent. Thus, using GenAI tools often mimics what it is like to engage with another human being. As humans, we generally enjoy social interaction, so it is understandable that GenAI experiences are powerful and hard to ignore.

Yet, as I have (hopefully) shown by now, GenAI tools do not think, they merely simulate thinking. All GenAI models, at their heart, are *simulacra*. They are pretenders designed to induce and sustain interaction with true intelligences (us). This is not inherently problematic, so long as the users and creators of GenAI tools acknowledge the fiction. It is, however, dangerous to position GenAI tools as quasi-human (or agentic) beings capable of pure cognition. We should all be suspicious of Silicon Valley elites who suggest otherwise, as they are knowingly spreading a fiction that serves their interests, their shareholders, and their bottom line more than it serves us.

Educators are at the front line of how humanity will deal with the seductive elements of GenAI tools. Although I have made a case for the practical use of GenAI in and beyond the classroom, it is still important to be wary of overuse, as there is currently little to no evidence that GenAI use leads to *better* learning outcomes for students. Indeed, the notion of better vs. worse outcomes is likely the wrong paradigm.

Instead, we should simply presume *different* outcomes and interrogate those differences against the goals we have set for ourselves and our children. Ideally, this should move beyond market pressures (i.e., ensuring that a child enters the labor force). Reducing education to the creation of labor is to deny large swaths of people what it means to be human. We are more than cogs in machines we do not own, but only if we allow ourselves to be—and hold those who would reduce us to commodities accountable for their actions.

This requires us to be wary of the frictionless experiences I have described, as they are small acts of seduction intended to capture our attention and record our cognition in ways that will enable it to be simulated later. All for the ultimate goal of generating wealth for others. Thus, though innocuous, I encourage everyone to use GenAI tools that are useful, but to be wary of the toolmakers' intentions, as they are not necessarily in your best interests.

I leave you with a final thought. In writing this book, I was reminded of this passage from C. S. Lewis's *The Screwtape Letters* (Lewis, 1942/2001), where an elder devil (Screwtape) corresponds with his nephew, a junior tempter (Wormwood):

> But do remember, the only thing that matters is the extent to which you separate the man from the Enemy. It does not matter how small the sins are provided that their cumulative effect is to edge the man away from the Light and out into the Nothing. Murder is no better than cards if cards can do the trick. Indeed the safest road to Hell is the gradual one—the gentle slope, soft underfoot, without sudden turnings, without milestones, without signposts,
>
> Your affectionate uncle
> SCREWTAPE

I am likely overstating my point by invoking devils in my concluding discussion of GenAI. Yet, if this imagery makes you uncomfortable, then I've accomplished my goal. We should always *wrestle* with discomfort in order to ensure that we act in accordance with our core values.

This is especially true as we consider how GenAI will fit into our educational experiences. Screwtape deftly argues the road to Hell is a scenic route that is comfortable and unnoticed by those that walk it . . . until they arrive at the final destination. Thus, small acts that undermine who we are lead to larger consequences that are difficult to walk back.

The use of GenAI tools can feel frictionless—this is by design. Yet, when we choose to not suffer through a task because "GenAI can do it," we should be mindful of what we lose. If the answer is "nothing important," then so be it. Yet, if the answer is "something that would have made me a stronger thinker," or "something that would have made the world a little better," then we should pause and reflect on whether or not the trade-off is worth the cost.

When we use GenAI tools for our own education—or for the education of others—we should acknowledge that we are walking down a path that leads *somewhere*. I conclude, then, that if the GenAI path is worth treading, then we should be well informed of the consequences of our journey. We should further acknowledge that overuse can lead us down a path of simulated intelligence that is of limited value to our continued intellectual development. Regardless of the path we choose, we should continue to fight for the process of *Authenticating Intelligence*, no matter how difficult the task becomes.

References

Abdelghani, R., Murayama, K., Kidd, C., Sauzéon, H., & Oudeyer, P. Y. (2025). Investigating middle school students question-asking and answer-evaluation skills when using ChatGPT for science investigation. *arXiv preprint* arXiv:2505.01106.

Adisa, I. O., & Adefisayo, A. O. (2025). Middle school students' perspectives on adopting generative AI in K-12 education. *The Journal of Educational Research, 118*(6), 1–12.

Adnin, R., Pandkar, A., Yao, B., Wang, D., & Das, M. (2025, April). Examining student and teacher perspectives on undisclosed use of generative AI in academic work. In *Proceedings of the 2025 CHI conference on human factors in computing systems (CHI' 25), April 26-May 1, Yokohama, Japan* (pp. 1–17).

Aguilar, S. J. (2018). Learning analytics: At the nexus of big data, digital innovation, and social justice in education. *TechTrends, 62*(1), 37–45.

Aguilar, S. J. (2020a). A research-based approach for evaluating resources for transitioning to teaching online. *Information and Learning Sciences, 121*(5/6), 301–310.

Aguilar, S. J. (2020b). Guidelines and tools for bridging the digital divide. *Information and Learning Sciences, 121*(5–6), 285–299.

Aguilar, S. J. (2022, March). Experimental evidence of performance feedback vs. mastery feedback on students' academic motivation. In *LAK22: 12th international learning analytics and knowledge conference* (pp. 556–562).

Aguilar, S. J. (2024a). *Authentic intelligence: Preventing AI from "Hijacking" education*. Keynote. Vermont State University. Burlington, VT.

Aguilar, S. J. (2024b). *Not a revolution, but a phase shift: AI and higher ed.* Keynote. Purdue University. West Lafayette, IN.

Aguilar, S. J. (2025). *Finding AI's place in your classroom*. Rimm of the World School District. Keynote. Lake Arrowhead, CA.

Aguilar, S. J., Galperin, H., Baek, C., & Gonzalez, E. (2022). Live instruction predicts engagement in K–12 remote learning. *Educational Researcher, 51*(1), 81–84.

Aguilar, S. J., Karabenick, S. A., Teasley, S. D., & Baek, C. (2021). Associations between learning analytics dashboard exposure and motivation and self-regulated learning. *Computers & Education, 162*, 104085.

Aguilar, S. J., Nye, B., Swartout, W. R., Macias, A., Xing, Y., & Xiu, R. (2025). *How students and teachers worldwide are adapting to AI.* https://doi.org/10.35542/osf.io/wr6n3_v3

Aguilar, S. J., Swartout, W., Nye, B., Sinatra, G. M., Wang, C., & Bui, E. (2024). Critical thinking and ethics in the age of generative AI in education. https://doi.org/10.35542/osf.io/7dr9j

Aguilar, S. J., & Wang, C. (2024). Duty vs. consequence: Exploring teachers' assessment of the ethical dimensions of generative AI technologies. In *Proceedings of ACM SAC Conference (SAC'24).* ACM, New York, NY, USA.

Allen, K. A., Jamshidi, N., Berger, E., Reupert, A., Wurf, G., & May, F. (2022). Impact of school-based interventions for building school belonging in adolescence: A systematic review. *Educational Psychology Review, 34*(1), 229–257.

Alexander, P. A. (2003). The development of expertise: The journey from acclimation to proficiency. *Educational Researcher, 32*(8), 10–14.

Alexander, P. A. (2005). The path to competence: A lifespan developmental perspective on reading. *Journal of Literacy Research, 37*(4), 413–436.

Al-Mashaqbeh, I. F. (2016). IPad in elementary school math learning setting. *International Journal of Emerging Technologies in Learning, 11*(2), 48.

Altick, R. D. (1998). *The English common reader: A social history of the mass reading public, 1800–1900.* The Ohio State University Press.

Amani, S., White, L., Balart, T., Arora, L., Shryock, K. J., Brumbelow, K., & Watson, K. L. (2023). Generative AI perceptions: A survey to measure the perceptions of faculty, staff, and students on generative AI tools in academia. *arXiv preprint* arXiv:2304.14415.

Andersen, J. F., Andersen, P. A., Murphy, M. A., & Wendt-Wasco, N. (1985). Teachers' reports of students' nonverbal communication in the classroom: A developmental study in grades K-12. *Communication Education, 34*(4), 292–307.

Anderson, J. R., Corbett, A. T., Koedinger, K. R., & Pelletier, R. (1995). Cognitive tutors: Lessons learned. *The Journal of the Learning Sciences, 4*(2), 167–207.

Anthropic. (2025). *Anthropic education report: How university students use claude.* https://www.anthropic.com/news/anthropic-education-report-how-university-students-use-claude

Apple. (2017). *An on-device deep neural network for face detection.* Apple Machine Learning Research. https://machinelearning.apple.com/research/face-detection

Artz, M., & Ren, Y. (2025). Beyond the GenAI gold rush: Mapping entrepreneurial tensions in the age of generative artificial intelligence. *Annals of Anthropological Practice*, *49*(1), e70016.

Aspiranti, K. B., & Larwin, K. H. (2021). Investigating the effects of tablet-based math interventions: A meta-analysis. *International Journal of Technology in Education and Science (IJTES)*, *5*(4), 629–647. https://doi.org/10.46328/ijtes.266

Atkisson, M., & Wiley, D. (2011, February). Learning analytics as interpretive practice: Applying Westerman to educational intervention. In *Proceedings of the 1st international conference on learning analytics and knowledge* (pp. 117–121) Banfff, AB, Canada.

Azenkot, S., Ladner, R. E., & Wobbrock, J. O. (2011, October). Smartphone haptic feedback for nonvisual wayfinding. In *The proceedings of the 13th international ACM SIGACCESS conference on Computers and accessibility* (pp. 281–282). Dundee, Scotland, UK.

Baek, C., & Aguilar, S. J. (2022). Past, present, and future directions of learning analytics research for students with disabilities. *Journal of Research on Technology in Education*, *55*(1), 1–16.

Baker, B. D., & Knight, D. (2025). *Does money matter in education?*. Albert Shanker Institute.

Baker, R. (2016). Using learning analytics in personalized learning. In M. Murphy, S. Redding, & J. Twyman (Eds.), *Handbook on personalized learning for states, districts, and schools* (pp. 165–174). Information Age Pub Inc.

Baker, R. S., Corbett, A. T., Koedinger, K. R., & Wagner, A. Z. (2004, April). Off-task behavior in the cognitive tutor classroom: When students "game the system". In *Proceedings of the SIGCHI conference on human factors in computing systems* (pp. 383–390). Vienna, Austria.

Baker, R. S., & Hawn, A. (2021). Algorithmic bias in education. *International Journal of Artificial Intelligence in Education*, 32, 1052–1092.

Barajas, J. (2025, August 19). Inside Cal State's big $17 million bet on ChatGPT for all. *LAist*. https://laist.com/news/education/chatgpt-california-state-university-csu-ai-deal

Bartolomé, A., Castañeda, L., & Adell, J. (2018). Personalisation in educational technology: The absence of underlying pedagogies. *International Journal of Educational Technology in Higher Education*, *15*(1), 14.

Bay, J. C. (1916). *Conrad Gesner (1516–1565) the father of bibliography* (Vol. 10, No. 2). Kraus Repr. Corporation.

Beckman, K., Apps, T., Howard, S. K., Rogerson, C., Rogerson, A., & Tondeur, J. (2025). The GenAI divide among university students: A call for action. *The Internet and Higher Education*, *67*, 101036.

Bender, E. M., & Koller, A. (2020, July). Climbing towards NLU: On meaning, form, and understanding in the age of data. In *Proceedings of the 58th annual meeting of the association for computational linguistics* (pp. 5185–5198).

Bertrand, M., & Mullainathan, S. (2004). Are Emily and Greg more employable than Lakisha and Jamal? A field experiment on labor market discrimination. *American Economic Review*, *94*(4), 991–1013.

Betthäuser, B. A., Bach-Mortensen, A. M., & Engzell, P. (2023). A systematic review and meta-analysis of the evidence on learning during the COVID-19 pandemic. *Nature Human Behaviour*, *7*(3), 375–385.

Biden, D. J. (2021, September 2). Jill Biden: A tribute to classroom heroes. *Time*. https://time.com/6094046/jill-biden-educators-essay/

Bitter, A. (2024, April 3). Amazon's Just Walk Out actually uses 1,000 people in India. *Business Insider*. https://www.businessinsider.com/amazons-just-walk-out-actually-1-000-people-in-india-2024-4

Bixler, S. (2019). One-to-one iPad technology in the middle school mathematics and science classrooms. *International Journal of Technology in Education and Science*, *3*(1), 1–18.

Bleemer, Z., & Mehta, A. (2022). Will studying economics make you rich? A regression discontinuity analysis of the returns to college major. *American Economic Journal: Applied Economics*, *14*(2), 1–22.

Blume, H. (2024, November 20). Founder of company that created LAUSD chatbot charted with fraud. *Los Angeles Times*. https://www.latimes.com/california/story/2024-11-19/founder-of-company-that-created-lausd-chatbot-charted-with-fraud

Borchers, C., Zhang, J., Baker, R. S., & Aleven, V. (2024, March). Using think-aloud data to understand relations between self-regulation cycle characteristics and student performance in intelligent tutoring systems. In *Proceedings of the 14th learning analytics and knowledge conference* (pp. 529–539). Kyoto, Japan.

Bourke, B. (2014). Positionality: Reflecting on the research process. *The Qualitative Report*, *19*(33), 1–9.

Brooks, C., Epp, C. D., Logan, G., & Greer, J. (2011, February). The who, what, when, and why of lecture capture. In *Proceedings of the 1st international conference on learning analytics and knowledge* (pp. 86–92). Banff, AB, Canada.

Brown, M. R., Higgins, K., Pierce, T., Hong, E., & Thoma, C. (2003). Secondary students' perceptions of school life with regard to alienation: The effects of disability, gender and race. *Learning Disability Quarterly*, *26*(4), 227–238.

Brown, T., Mann, B., Ryder, N., Subbiah, M., Kaplan, J. D., Dhariwal, P., ... & Amodei, D. (2020). Language models are few-shot learners. *Advances in Neural Information Processing Systems*, *33*, 1877–1901.

Browne, R. (2025, August 11). Sam Altman now says AGI, or human-level AI, is "not a super useful term" — and he's not alone. *CNBC*. https://www.cnbc.com/2025/08/11/sam-altman-says-agi-is-a-pointless-term-experts-agree.html

Bryant, J., Dorn, E., Hall, S., & Panier, F. (2020). Reimagining a more equitable and resilient K–12 education system. *McKinsey Insights*, 1–8. https://www.mckinsey.com/industries/education/our-insights/reimagining-a-more-equitable-and-resilient-k-12-education-system#

Bueie, A. A., Skar, G. B., & Graham, S. (2025). High school students' use and beliefs about generative artificial intelligence and writing in school. *Reading and Writing: An Interdisciplinary Journal*, 1–31. https://doi.org/10.1007/s11145-025-10702-3

Cammaerts, B. (2015). Social media and activism. *Journalism*, 1027–1034.

Campion, L. L. (2020). Leading through the enrollment cliff of 2026 (Part I). *TechTrends*, *64*(3), 542–544.

Carayon, P. (2006). Human factors of complex sociotechnical systems. *Applied Ergonomics*, *37*(4), 525–535.

Carr, J. M. (2012). Does math achievement h'APP'en when iPads and game-based learning are incorporated into fifth-grade mathematics instruction?. *Journal of Information Technology Education: Research*, *11*(1), 269–286.

Castilla, E. J., & Poskanzer, E. J. (2022). Through the front door: Why do organizations (still) prefer legacy applicants?. *American Sociological Review*, *87*(5), 782–826.

CDC. (2024, July 8). *CDC Museum COVID-19 timeline*. Centers for Disease Control and Prevention. https://www.cdc.gov/museum/timeline/covid19.html

Cerf, V. G. (2004). On the evolution of Internet technologies. *Proceedings of the IEEE*, *92*(9), 1360–1370.

Cervantes, M. (2016/1605). *Don quixote*. Simon and Schuster.

Chai, F., Ma, J., Wang, Y., Zhu, J., & Han, T. (2024). Grading by AI makes me feel fairer? How different evaluators affect college students' perception of fairness. *Frontiers in Psychology*, *15*, 1221177.

Chan, C. K. Y., & Lee, K. K. (2025). The balancing act between AI and authenticity in assessment: A case study of secondary school students' use of GenAI in reflective writing. *Computers & Education, 238*, 105399.

Chen, A. (2024). The relationship between family socioeconomic status and online education usage: A data analysis based on K-12 students. *Journal of Educational Research and Practice, 2*(3), 339–350.

Chen, C. (2025). Cultivating motivation in informal learning via YouTube: Effects of reinforcement learning-based and social learning-based approaches. *Learning and Motivation, 90*, 102122.

Chingos, M. M. (2013). Class size and student outcomes: Research and policy implications. *Journal of Policy Analysis and Management, 32*(2), 411–438.

Cho, C., & Ofosu-Anim, D. (2025). Exploring international students' perceptions of adopting generative artificial intelligence (GenAI) technologies in learning. *Social Sciences & Humanities Open, 11*, 101418.

Cohodes, S., Goldhaber, D., Hill, P., Ho, A., Kogan, V., Polikoff, M., ... & West, M. (2022). Student achievement gaps and the pandemic: A new review of evidence from 2021–2022. *Center on Reinventing Public Education.*

Collier, R. B., Dubal, V. B., & Carter, C. L. (2018). Disrupting regulation, regulating disruption: The politics of Uber in the United States. *Perspectives on Politics, 16*(4), 919–937.

Connelly, V., Campbell, S., MacLean, M., & Barnes, J. (2006). Contribution of lower order skills to the written composition of college students with and without dyslexia. *Developmental Neuropsychology, 29*(1), 175–196.

Connelly*, V., Dockrell, J. E., & Barnett, J. (2005). The slow handwriting of undergraduate students constrains overall performance in exam essays. *Educational Psychology, 25*(1), 99–107.

Cooper, R., & Foster, M. (1971). Sociotechnical systems. *American Psychologist, 26*(5), 467.

Corbett, A. T., Koedinger, K., & Hadley, W. S. (2001). Cognitive tutors: From the research classroom to all classrooms. In *Technology enhanced learning* (pp. 215–240). Routledge.

Corbin, T., Dawson, P., & Liu, D. (2025). Talk is cheap: Why structural assessment changes are needed for a time of GenAI. *Assessment & Evaluation in Higher Education*, 1–11.

Correa, N., & First, J. M. (2021). Examining the mental health impacts of COVID-19 on K-12 mental health providers, school teachers, and students. *Journal of School Counseling, 19*(42), n42.

Cotton, D. R., Cotton, P. A., & Shipway, J. R. (2024). Chatting and cheating: Ensuring academic integrity in the era of ChatGPT. *Innovations in Education and Teaching International*, *61*(2), 228–239.

Csikszentmihalyi, M., Abuhamdeh, S., & Nakamura, J. (2014). Flow. In *Flow and the foundations of positive psychology: The collected works of Mihaly Csikszentmihalyi* (pp. 227–238). Springer Netherlands.

Cutter, C. (2025, August 2). AI is coming for the consultants. Inside McKinsey, "This is existential." *The Wall Street Journal*. https://www.wsj.com/tech/ai/mckinsey-consulting-firms-ai-strategy-89fbf1be

Dabirian, A., Swarat, C., & Swarat, S. (2025). Necessary but not perfect: Changes in AI perception at a large university. *IT Professional*, *27*(4), 13–18.

Dai, Y. (2025). Why students use or not use generative AI: Student conceptions, concerns, and implications for engineering education. *Digital Engineering*, *4*, 100019.

Darling-Hammond, L. (2000). Teacher quality and student achievement. *Education Policy Analysis Archives*, *8*, 1–1.

de Fine Licht, K. (2024). Generative artificial intelligence in higher education: Why the 'banning approach' to student use is sometimes morally justified. *Philosophy & Technology*, *37*(3), 113.

Deci, E. L., & Ryan, R. M. (2012). Self-determination theory. In P. A. M. Van Lange, A. W. Kruglanski, & E. T. Higgins (Eds.), *Handbook of theories of social psychology* (pp. 416–436). Sage Publications Ltd.

Dellinger, H., & Walker, M. (2025, July 24). Amid questions over ChatGPT use, Detroit school board candidate withdraws. *Chalkbeat*. https://www.chalkbeat.org/detroit/2025/07/24/detroit-school-board-candidate-withdraws-as-questions-raised-about-chatgpt/

Demirjian, K., & Nehamas, N. (2025, September 25). Democratic report says disorder at DOGE Jeopardized Americans' data. *The New York Times*. https://www.nytimes.com/2025/09/25/us/politics/democratic-report-disorder-doge.html

Denoyelles, A., Brown, T., Seilhamer, R., & Chen, B. (2023, January 25). The evolving landscape of students' mobile learning practices in higher education. *EDUCAUSE Review*. https://er.educause.edu/articles/2023/1/the-evolving-landscape-of-students-mobile-learning-practices-in-higher-education

Derby, S., & Richardson, J. V. (2001). Encarta: The reference tool of the future?. *The Library quarterly* (Chicago, IL), *71*(2), 261–269.

Descartes, R. (1641/2008). *Meditations on first philosophy: With selections from the objections and replies*. Oxford University Press.

Desmedt, C. P., Budts, W., De Vos, M., & Moons, P. (2025). Artificial intelligence-generated podcasts open new doors to make science accessible: A mixed-method evaluation of quality and the potential for science communication. *European Journal of Cardiovascular Nursing, 24*(6): 885–895.

Detroit Public Schools Community District Board. (2025). Board of Education / Board Vacancy Questionnaire. *Detroitk12.org*. https://www.detroitk12.org/Page/18859

Dewey, J. (1998/1938). What I believe. In L. A. Hickman & T. M. Alexander (Eds.), *The essential Dewey: Vol. 1. Pragmatism, education, democracy*. Indiana University Press (pp. 22). (Original work published 1938)

Digital Divide Slugfest. (2002, February 6). *Cbsnews.com*. https://www.cbsnews.com/news/digital-divide-slugfest/

Dorn, E., Hancock, B., Sarakatsannis, J., & Viruleg, E. (2020). COVID-19 and student learning in the United States: The hurt could last a lifetime. *McKinsey & Company, 1*(1), 1–9.

Druckman, J. N., Levy, J., & Sands, N. (2021). Bias in education disability accommodations. *Economics of Education Review, 85*, 102176.

Dubois, D. (2024). Paradoxes of generative AI: Both promise and threat to academic freedom. *AAUP Journal of Academic Freedom, 15.*

Earnest, E. (1958). Must the TV technicians take over the colleges?. *AAUP Bulletin, 44*(3), 582–588.

Easley, G. (2025, September 25). Reimagining school in the age of AI. *NOEMA*. https://www.noemamag.com/reimagining-school-in-the-age-of-ai/

Eaton, S. E. (2023). Postplagiarism: Transdisciplinary ethics and integrity in the age of artificial intelligence and neurotechnology. *International Journal for Educational Integrity, 19*(1), 23. https://doi.org/10.1007/s40979-023-00144-1

Eg, R., Tønnesen, Ö. D., & Tennfjord, M. K. (2023). A scoping review of personalized user experiences on social media: The interplay between algorithms and human factors. *Computers in Human Behavior Reports, 9*, 100253.

Ehrenberg, R. G., Brewer, D. J., Gamoran, A., & Willms, J. D. (2001). Class size and student achievement. *Psychological Science in the Public Interest, 2*(1), 1–30.

Ellington, A. J. (2003). A meta-analysis of the effects of calculators on students' achievement and attitude levels in precollege mathematics classes. *Journal for Research in Mathematics Education, 34*(5), 433–463.

Engzell, P., Frey, A., & Verhagen, M. D. (2021). Learning loss due to school closures during the COVID-19 pandemic. *Proceedings of the National Academy of Sciences, 118*(17), e2022376118.

Fan, Y., Tang, L., Le, H., Shen, K., Tan, S., Zhao, Y., ... & Gašević, D. (2025). Beware of metacognitive laziness: Effects of generative artificial intelligence on learning motivation, processes, and performance. *British Journal of Educational Technology, 56*(2), 489–530.

Fancsali, S. E. (2011, February). Variable construction for predictive and causal modeling of online education data. In *Proceedings of the 1st international conference on learning analytics and knowledge* (pp. 54–63). Banff, AB, Canada.

Fayaza, M. F., Senthilrajah, T., Wijesinghe, U., & Ahangama, S. (2025, February). Role of GenAI in student knowledge enhancement: Learner perception. In *2025 5th International Conference on Advanced Research in Computing (ICARC)* (pp. 1–6). IEEE.

Fenton, A. (2024). Reconsidering the use of oral exams and assessments: An old way to move into a new future. *Educational Researcher, 54*(7), 430–436.

Ferguson, C. H. (2004). *The broadband problem: Anatomy of a market failure and a policy dilemma*. Rowman & Littlefield.

Feuerriegel, S., Hartmann, J., Janiesch, C., & Zschech, P. (2024). Generative AI. *Business & Information Systems Engineering, 66*(1), 111–126.

Field, H. (2025, April 3). OpenAI, Anthropic target college students with latest education AI announcements. *CNBC*. https://www.cnbc.com/2025/04/03/openai-anthropic-target-college-students-with-education-ai-services.html

Fields, M., & Liu, Y. (2025). College student opinions on generative artificial intelligence for educational experiences. In *Proceedings of the* human factors *and* ergonomics society annual meeting (p. 10711813251367749). Chicago, IL. SAGE Publications.

FitzGerald, E., Kucirkova, N., Jones, A., Cross, S., Ferguson, R., Herodotou, C., ... & Scanlon, E. (2018). Dimensions of personalisation in technology-enhanced learning: A framework and implications for design. *British Journal of Educational Technology, 49*(1), 165–181.

Fosnot, C. T. (2013). *Constructivism: Theory, perspectives, and practice.* Teachers College Press.

Frazier, M., & Hearrington, D. (2024). *The technology coordinator's handbook: A guide for Edtech facilitators and leaders*. ASCD.

Freedman, A. (2025, June 20). OpenAI CEO says his kids will "never be smarter than AI"— and that his parenting style relies on ChatGPT.

Fortune Well; *Fortune*. https://fortune.com/well/2025/06/20/sam-altman-openai-ceo-parenting-kids-ai/

Friedman, J. (2024, October 21). How snake oil became a symbol of fraud and deception. *Smithsonian Magazine*. https://www.smithsonianmag.com/innovation/how-snake-oil-became-a-symbol-of-fraud-and-deception-180985300/

Fuller, S. C., Swiderski, T., Mikkelsen, C., & Bastian, K. C. (2025). In school, engaged, on track? The effect of the pandemic on student attendance, course grades, and grade retention in North Carolina. *Educational Researcher*, *54*(2), 78–90.

Fulmer, S. M., & Frijters, J. C. (2009). A review of self-report and alternative approaches in the measurement of student motivation. *Educational Psychology Review*, *21*(3), 219–246.

Galusha, J. M. (1997). Barriers to learning in distance education. *Interpersonal Computing and Technology*, *5*(3/4), 6–14. https://www.learntechlib.org/ p/85240/

Garner, J. (2025, April 9). Helping educators reimagine AI's role in transformational learning. *EdSurge*. https://www.edsurge.com/news/2025-04-09-helping-educators-reimagine-ai-s-role-in-transformational-learning

Gecker, J. (2023, August 10). Paper exams, chatbot bans: Colleges seek to "ChatGPT-proof" assignments. *AP News*. https://apnews.com/article/chatgpt-cheating-ai-college-1b654b44de2d0dfa4e50bf0186137fc1

Gessner, C. (1545). *Bibliotheca universalis*. Christoph Froschauer

Gibbs, K. (2023). Voices in practice: Challenges to implementing differentiated instruction by teachers and school leaders in an Australian mainstream secondary school. *The Australian Educational Researcher*, *50*(4), 1217–1232.

Gibson, K. R., & Ingold, T. (Eds.). (1993). *Tools, language and cognition in human evolution*. Cambridge University Press.

Gilreath, A. (2025, June 19). To employers, AI skills aren't just for tech majors anymore. *The Hechinger Report*. https://hechingerreport.org/to-employers-ai-skills-arent-just-for-tech-majors-anymore/

Giles, C., Boland Chira, S., Garrett-Ostermiller, D., Garrett-Ostermiller, J., Harrington, S., Sherriff, G., ... & Thompson, J. (2025). *Exploring faculty, student, and staff perceptions of Generative AI through a civic learning project for first-year engineering and mathematical sciences students.*

Giordano, V. (2023, October 20). How many books are in the world? (2025). *ISBNDB Blog*. https://isbndb.com/blog/how-many-books-are-in-the-world/

Glazer, N. (2014). Formative plus summative assessment in large undergraduate courses: Why both?. *International Journal of Teaching and Learning in Higher Education*, *26*(2), 276–286.

Goldstein, A. (2024, September 18). Harnessing AI's potential to lift up underserved communities – California health care foundation. *California Health Care Foundation*. https://www.chcf.org/resource/harnessing-ais-potential-lift-up-underserved-communities/

Grannell, C. (2010, December 30). The school that gives every student an iPad. *TechRadar*. https://www.techradar.com/news/computing/apple/the-school-that-gives-every-student-an-ipad-915539

Graves, J. M., Abshire, D. A., Amiri, S., & Mackelprang, J. L. (2021). Disparities in technology and broadband internet access across rurality: Implications for health and education. *Family & Community Health*, *44*(4), 257–265.

Guest, O., Suarez, M., Müller, B., van Meerkerk, E., Oude Groote Beverborg, A., de Haan, R., Reyes Elizondo, A., Blokpoel, M., Scharfenberg, N., Kleinherenbrink, A., Camerino, I., Woensdregt, M., Monett, D., Brown, J., Avraamidou, L., Alenda-Demoutiez, J., Hermans, F., & van Rooij, I. (2025). Against the uncritical aadoption of 'AI' technologies in academia. *Zenodo*. https://doi.org/10.5281/zenodo.17065099

Hak, J., Johnson, N. L., Amoozadeh, M., Alipour, A., & Chattopadhyay, S. (2025). Observing without doing: Pseudo-apprenticeship patterns in student LLM use. In *Proceedings of the 25th Koli Calling International Conference on Computing Education Research (Koli Calling' 25), November 11–16, 2025, Koli, Finland* (pp. 1–11). ACM, New York, NY, USA. https://doi.org/10.1145/3769994.3770027

Hallas, L., Hatibie, A., Majumdar, S., Pyarali, M., & Hale, T. (2021). *Variation in US states' responses to COVID-19*. University of Oxford.

Halloran, C., Jack, R., Okun, J. C., & Oster, E. (2021). *Pandemic schooling mode and student test scores: Evidence from US states* (No. w29497). National Bureau of Economic Research.

Halverson, A. (2025, September 8). Microsoft layoffs continue into 5th consecutive month. *The Seattle Times*. https://www.seattletimes.com/business/microsoft/microsoft-layoffs-continue-into-5th-consecutive-month/

Hausfather, S. J. (1996). Vygotsky and schooling: Creating a social context for learning. *Action in Teacher Education*, *18*(2), 1–10.

Heidegger, M. (1962). *Being and time* (Macquarrie and Robinson, Trans.). Harper and Row.

Heffernan, N. T., & Heffernan, C. L. (2014). The ASSISTments ecosystem: Building a platform that brings scientists and teachers together for minimally invasive research on human learning and teaching. *International Journal of Artificial Intelligence in Education*, *24*(4), 470–497.

Heffernan, T. (2022). Sexism, racism, prejudice, and bias: A literature review and synthesis of research surrounding student evaluations of courses and teaching. *Assessment & Evaluation in Higher Education*, *47*(1), 144–154.

Helal, M. Y., Elgendy, I. A., Albashrawi, M. A., Dwivedi, Y. K., Al-Ahmadi, M. S., & Jeon, I. (2025). The impact of generative AI on critical thinking skills: A systematic review, conceptual framework and future research directions. *Information Discovery and Delivery*.

Hewes, G. W. (1993). A history of speculation on the relation between tools and language. In K. R. Gibson & T. Ingold (Eds.), *Tools, language, and cognition in human evolution* (pp. 20–31). Cambridge University Press.

Hidayat, M. T. (2024). Effectiveness of AI-based personalised reading platforms in enhancing reading comprehension. *Journal of Learning for Development*, *11*(1), 115–125.

Howe, C., Hennessy, S., Mercer, N., Vrikki, M., & Wheatley, L. (2019). Teacher–student dialogue during classroom teaching: Does it really impact on student outcomes?. *Journal of the Learning Sciences*, *28*(4–5), 462–512.

Huang, D., Hash, N., Cummings, J. J., & Prena, K. (2025). Academic cheating with generative AI: Exploring a moral extension of the theory of planned behavior. *Computers and Education: Artificial Intelligence*, *8*, 100424.

Hyde, M. (2025, August). Use of AI in airlines ticket pricing raise concerns. *NPR*. https://www.npr.org/2025/08/01/nx-s1-5479180/use-of-ai-in-airlines-ticket-pricing-raise-concerns

Ibarra, B. N. (2022). Understanding SEL to create a sense of belonging: The role teachers play in addressing students' social and emotional well-being. *Current Issues in Education*, *23*(2).

Isaacs, A. M., & Chan, B. (2020). *Zoom: The challenge of scaling with COVID-19 on the horizon (A)*. The Berkeley-Haas Case Series. University of California, Berkeley, Haas School of Business.

Jacobs, I., & Osvath, M. (2023). Tool use and tooling in ravens (Corvus corax): A review and novel observations. *Ethology*, *129*(3), 169–181.

Järvelä, S., Zhao, G., Nguyen, A., & Chen, H. (2025). Hybrid intelligence: Human–AI coevolution and learning. *British Journal of Educational Technology*, *56*(2), 455–468.

Jenkinson, J. (2000). All students belong: Inclusive education for students with severe learning disabilities. *Tizard Learning Disability Review*, *5*(4), 4–13.

Jiang, Y., Xie, L., & Cao, X. (2025). Exploring the effectiveness of institutional policies and regulations for generative AI usage in higher education. *Higher Education Quarterly*, *79*(4), e70054.

Johnson, K. (2024, August 6). California's two biggest school districts botched AI deals. Here are lessons from their mistakes. *CalMatters*. https://calmatters.org/economy/technology/2024/08/botched-ai-education-deals-lessons/

Johnson, N. N., Johnson, T. L., & McCurdy, D. (2024). Artificial intelligence, academic freedom, and the evolving debate over forgery and truth in the twenty-first century. *AAUP Journal of Academic Freedom*.

Johri, A., Schleiss, J., & Ranade, N. (2025, April). Lessons for GenAI literacy from a field study of Human-GenAI augmentation in the workplace. In *2025 IEEE Global Engineering Education Conference (EDUCON)* (pp. 1–9). IEEE.

Jones II, A. (2025, September 4). Artificial intelligence is here. Will it replace teachers? *ABC News*. https://abcnews.go.com/Politics/artificial-intelligence-replace-teachers/story?id=12516305

Joosten, J., Bilgram, V., Hahn, A., & Totzek, D. (2024). Comparing the ideation quality of humans with generative artificial intelligence. *IEEE Engineering Management Review*, *52*(2), 153–164.

Joshi, S. (2025a). Bridging the AI skills gap: Workforce training for financial services. Available at *SSRN* 5206490.

Joshi, S. (2025b). The transformative role of agentic GenAI in shaping workforce development and education in the US. Available at *SSRN* 5133376.

Judge, S., Puckett, K., & Cabuk, B. (2004). Digital equity: New findings from the early childhood longitudinal study. *Journal of Research on Technology in Education*, *36*(4), 383–396.

Kahney, L. (1999, June 4). Flying car set for takeoff. *WIRED*. https://www.wired.com/1999/06/flying-car-set-for-takeoff/

Kant, I. (1998/1785). *Groundwork of the metaphysics of morals* (M. Gregor, Trans.). Cambridge University Press.

Kangwa, D., Msafiri, M. M., & Fute, A. (2025). Exploring the factors that promote a balance between academic integrity and the effective use of GenAI tools in higher education: A systematic review. *Journal of Computer Assisted Learning*, *41*(5), e70109.

Kaplan, J., McCandlish, S., Henighan, T., Brown, T. B., Chess, B., Child, R., ... & Amodei, D. (2020). Scaling laws for neural language models. *arXiv* preprint arXiv:2001.08361.

Karl, K. A., Peluchette, J. V., & Aghakhani, N. (2022). Virtual work meetings during the COVID-19 pandemic: The good, bad, and ugly. *Small Group Research*, *53*(3), 343–365.

Kass, S. J., Cole, K. S., & Stanny, C. J. (2007). Effects of distraction and experience on situation awareness and simulated driving. *Transportation Research Part F: Traffic Psychology and Behaviour*, *10*(4), 321–329.

Kastrenakes, J. (2023, August 14). Amazon adds AI-generated review summaries so you don't have to read the comments. *The Verge*. https://www.theverge.com/2023/8/14/23831391/amazon-review-summaries-generative-ai

Keppler, S., Sinchaisri, W. P., & Snyder, C. (2025). Backwards planning with generative ai: Case study evidence from us k12 teachers. Available at SSRN 4924786.

Kirkpatrick, L., Brown, H. M., Searle, M., Smyth, R. E., Ready, E. A., & Kennedy, K. (2018). Impact of a one-to-one iPad initiative on grade 7 students' achievement in language arts, mathematics, and learning skills. *Computers in the Schools*, *35*(3), 171–185.

Klopfer, E., Reich, J., Abelson, H., & Breazeal, C. (2024). Generative AI and K-12 education: An MIT perspective. *An MIT exploration of generative AI*. https://doi.org/10.21428/e4baedd9.81164b06

Knuth, D. E. (1997). *The art of computer programming* (Vol. 3). Pearson Education.

Koenig, R. (2021, October 27). The pandemic pushed colleges to record lectures. The practice may be here to stay. *EdSurge*. https://www.edsurge.com/news/2021-10-27-the-pandemic-pushed-colleges-to-record-lectures-the-practice-may-be-here-to-stay

Kordzadeh, N., & Ghasemaghaei, M. (2022). Algorithmic bias: Review, synthesis, and future research directions. *European Journal of Information Systems*, *31*(3), 388–409.

Kubulan, C. (2025). Summer conference offers faculty and staff opportunity to reimagine education with AI. *Cpp.edu*. https://www.cpp.edu/news/content/2025/04/summer-conference-offers-faculty-and-staff-opportunity-to-reimagine-education-with-ai/index.shtml

Kuhlmann, D. O., & Ardichvili, A. (2015). Becoming an expert: Developing expertise in an applied discipline. *European Journal of Training and Development*, *39*(4), 262–276.

Laak, K. J., Abdelghani, R., & Aru, J. (2024, July). Personalisation is not guaranteed: The challenges of using generative AI for personalised learning. In *International conference on innovative technologies and learning* (pp. 40–49). Springer Nature Switzerland.

Lambert, J., & Stevens, M. (2024). ChatGPT and generative AI technology: A mixed bag of concerns and new opportunities. *Computers in the Schools, 41*(4), 559–583.

Lapowsky, I. (2015, May 8). What schools must learn from LA's iPad debacle. *WIRED*. https://www.wired.com/2015/05/los-angeles-edtech/

Lee, H. P., Sarkar, A., Tankelevitch, L., Drosos, I., Rintel, S., Banks, R., & Wilson, N. (2025, April). The impact of generative AI on critical thinking: Self-reported reductions in cognitive effort and confidence effects from a survey of knowledge workers. In *Proceedings of the 2025 CHI conference on human factors in computing systems* (pp. 1–22). Yokohama, Japan.

Lee, V. R. (2025, September 4). I study AI cheating. Here's what the data actually says. *Vox*. https://www.vox.com/technology/458875/ai-cheating-data-education-panic

Leech, N. L., Gullett, S., Cummings, M. H., & Haug, C. A. (2022). The challenges of remote K-12 education during the COVID-19 pandemic: Differences by grade level. *Online Learning, 26*(1), 245–267.

Leitner, P., Khalil, M., & Ebner, M. (2017). Learning analytics in higher education—a literature review. In A. Peña-Ayala (Ed.), *Learning analytics: Fundaments, applications, and trends* (pp. 1–23). Springer.

Lewis, C. S. (1942/2001). *The screwtape letters*. Zondervan.

Li, F., Ziegler, H., Gonzales, A., Galloway, E. P., & Wise, A. F. (2025a). A socio-cultural approach to personalization in education: Case studies in empowering learners as knowers with AI. In *Proceedings of the 19th International Conference of the Learning Sciences-ICLS 2025* (pp. 1704–1708). International Society of the Learning Sciences. Helsinki, Finland.

Li, S., & Wang, W. (2022). Effect of blended learning on student performance in K-12 settings: A meta-analysis. *Journal of Computer Assisted Learning, 38*(5), 1254–1272.

Li, T., & Iacobelli, F. (2023, October). Purposeful AI. In *Companion publication of the 2023 conference on computer supported cooperative work and social computing* (pp. 563–565).

Li, T., Zhan, Z., Ji, Y., & Li, T. (2025b). Exploring human and AI collaboration in inclusive STEM teacher training: A synergistic approach based on self-determination theory. *The Internet and Higher Education, 65*, 101003.

Li, Y., Shan, Z., Raković, M., Guan, Q., Gašević, D., & Chen, G. (2025c). When AI explains in natural language: Unveiling the impact of generative AI explanations on educators' grading and feedback practices. *Education and Information Technologies*, 1–34. https://doi.org/10.1007/s10639-025-13741-z

Lichand, G., Dória, C. A., Neto, O. L., & Cossi, J. (2021). The impacts of remote learning in secondary education: Evidence from Brazil during the pandemic. *Nature Human Behaviour*, *6*, 1079–1086.

Lichtenberg, N. (2025, September 7). This Stanford computer science professor went to written exams 2 years ago because of AI. He says his students insisted on it. *Yahoo News*. https://www.yahoo.com/news/articles/stanford-computer-science-professor-went-093500264.html

Lin, L., & Pinnameneni, A. (2025, September 5). Duke University pilot project examining pros and cons of using artificial intelligence in college. *AP News*. https://apnews.com/article/artificial-intelligence-colleges-and-universities-alice-mary-baldwin-general-news-e0037fe9d6731010894bb6d4b52f9665

Liu, X., Guo, B., He, W., & Hu, X. (2025). Effects of generative artificial intelligence on K-12 and higher education students' learning outcomes: A meta-analysis. *Journal of Educational Computing Research*, *63*(5), 1249–1291.

Lonn, S., Aguilar, S. J., & Teasley, S. D. (2015). Investigating student motivation in the context of a learning analytics intervention during a summer bridge program. *Computers in Human Behavior*, *47*, 90–97.

Luo, J. (2024). A critical review of GenAI policies in higher education assessment: A call to reconsider the "originality" of students' work. *Assessment & Evaluation in Higher Education*, *49*(5), 651–664.

Macias, A., & Aguilar, S. J. (2026). Ask or outsource? What drives students to use GenAI strategically (or reliantly). In *Proceedings of the 2025 connected learning summit*. Online.

Mack, M. B. (2025, June 3). AI startup backed by Microsoft revealed to be 700 Indian employees pretending to be chatbots. *Latin Times*. https://www.latintimes.com/ai-startup-backed-microsoft-revealed-700-indian-employees-pretending-chatbots-584240

Madden, M., Calvin, A., Hasse, A., & Lenhart, A. (2024). *The dawn of the AI era: Teens, parents, and the adoption of generative AI at home and school*. Common Sense.

Magic School, Inc. (n.d.). *MagicSchool: The AI platform for educators* [Web page]. https://www.magicschool.ai

Major, L., Francis, G. A., & Tsapali, M. (2021). The effectiveness of technology-supported personalised learning in low-and middle-income countries: A meta-analysis. *British Journal of Educational Technology*, *52*(5), 1935–1964.

Marcinkowski, F., Kieslich, K., Starke, C., & Lünich, M. (2020, January). Implications of AI (un-) fairness in higher education admissions: The effects of perceived AI (un-) fairness on exit, voice and organizational reputation. In *Proceedings of the 2020 conference on fairness, accountability, and transparency* (pp. 122–130). Barcelona, Spain.

Marr, B. (2025, July 8). Microsoft makes AI mandatory for employees: What it means for your career. *Forbes*. https://www.forbes.com/sites/bernardmarr/2025/07/08/microsoft-makes-ai-mandatory-for-employees-what-it-means-for-your-career/

Mathewson, T. G. (2020, April 23). Coronavirus opens doors to rethinking education. *The Hechinger Report*. https://hechingerreport.org/coronavirus-opens-doors-to-rethinking-education/

Mathewson, T. G. (2023, August 14). AI detection tools falsely accuse international students of cheating. *The Markup*. https://themarkup.org/machine-learning/2023/08/14/ai-detection-tools-falsely-accuse-international-students-of-cheating

Mathewson, T. G. (2025, June 26). Turnitin helps colleges detect AI writing — but its cost is more than just a price tag. *CalMatters*. https://calmatters.org/education/higher-education/2025/06/ai-detector/

Matute, M. (2001, February 11). Latinos and the digital divide. *Los Angeles Times*. https://www.latimes.com/archives/la-xpm-2001-feb-11-me-24169-story.html

Maxwell, D., Oyarzun, B., Kim, S., & Bong, J. Y. (2025). Generative AI in higher education: Demographic differences in student perceived readiness, benefits, and challenges. *TechTrends*, *69*, 1248–1259.

Mayer, A. S., Baygi, R. M., & Buwalda, R. (2025). Generation AI: Job crafting by entry-level professionals in the age of generative AI: A.-S. Mayer et al. *Business & Information Systems Engineering*, *67*, 595–613.

McCrea, B. (2010). Measuring the iPad's potential for education. *THE Journal*. https://thejournal.com/articles/2010/01/27/measuring-the-ipads-potential-for-education.aspx

McDonald, N., Johri, A., Ali, A., & Collier, A. H. (2025). Generative artificial intelligence in higher education: Evidence from an analysis of institutional policies and guidelines. *Computers in Human Behavior: Artificial Humans*, *3*, 100121.

McGraw-Hill Education. (2015, March 9). *Report: New McGraw-Hill education research finds more than 80 percent of students use mobile technology to study*. https://www.prnewswire.com/news-releases/report-new-mcgraw-hill-education-research-finds-more-than-80-percent-of-students-use-mobile-technology-to-study-300047130.html

McMurtrie, B.(2024, November 4). Cheating has become normal. *The Chronicle of Higher Education*. https://www.chronicle.com/article/cheating-has-become-normal

Means, B., Toyama, Y., Murphy, R., & Baki, M. (2013). The effectiveness of online and blended learning: A meta-analysis of the empirical literature. *Teachers College Record*, *115*(3), 1–47.

Mearian, L. (2025, May 6). IBM CEO: Smaller, domain-specific genAI models are the future. *Computerworld*. https://www.computerworld.com/article/3978675/ibm-ceo-smaller-domain-specific-genai-models-are-the-future.html

Mehmet, M., Papakosmas, M., Kyriazis, E., & Nikidehaghani, M. (2025). Re-imagining marketing education for career readiness in the GenAI era. *Journal of Marketing Education*, *47*(2), 170–190.

Meske, C., Hermanns, T., von der Weiden, E., Loser, K. U., & Berger, T. (2025). Vibe coding as a reconfiguration of intent mediation in software development: Definition, implications, and research agenda. *arXiv preprint* arXiv:2507.21928.

Middleton, K. L., & Chambers, V. (2010). Approaching digital equity: Is wifi the new leveler?. *Information Technology & People*, *23*(1), 4–22.

Mill, J. S. (2016). *Utilitarianism*. In *Seven masterpieces of philosophy* (pp. 329–375). Routledge.

Minaya, V., & Scott-Clayton, J. (2022). Labor market trajectories for community college graduates: How returns to certificates and associate's degrees evolve over time. *Education Finance and Policy*, *17*(1), 53–80.

Mishra, P. (2025). Brains without minds: Musings on visual literacy and GenAI. *Journal of Visual Literacy*, *44*(3), 1–15.

Moje, E. B. (1996). "I teach students, not subjects": Teacher-student relationships as contexts for secondary literacy. *Reading Research Quarterly*, *31*(2), 172–195.

Moscoviz, L., & Evans, D. K. (2022). *Learning loss and student dropouts during the covid-19 pandemic: A review of the evidence two years after schools shut down*. Center for Global Development.

Muris, P., Merckelbach, H., Otgaar, H., & Meijer, E. (2017). The Malevolent side of human nature: A meta-analysis and critical review of the literature on the Dark Triad (Narcissism, Machiavellianism, and Psychopathy). *Perspectives on Psychological Science*, *12*(2), 183–204.

Myrick, J. G. (2015). Emotion regulation, procrastination, and watching cat videos online: Who watches Internet cats, why, and to what effect?. *Computers in Human Behavior*, *52*, 168–176.

National Academies of Sciences, Medicine, Division of Behavioral, Social Sciences, Board on Science Education, Board on Behavioral, ... & Practice of Learning. (2018). *How people learn II: Learners, contexts, and cultures*. National Academies Press.

Nelson, A. S., Santamaría, P. V., Javens, J. S., & Ricaurte, M. (2025). Students' perceptions of generative artificial intelligence (GenAI) Use in academic writing in english as a foreign language. *Education Sciences*, *15*(5), 611.

Nix, T., Pendergast, D., & O'Brien, M. (2022). Belonging in school–The effect of teacher-student relationships: A systematic quantitative review of the literature. *Education Thinking*, *2*(1), 63–90.

Noble, S. U. (2018). *Algorithms of oppression: How search engines reinforce racism*. New York University Press.

Norberg, K., Murphy, A., De Ley, L., Moltz, E. S., Almoubayyed, H., & Ritter, S. (2025, July). Using generative AI to foster student sense of belonging in mathematics. In *International conference on artificial intelligence in education* (pp. 188–195). Springer Nature Switzerland.

Norman, D. (2013). T*he design of everyday things: Revised and expanded edition*. Basic books.

Novak, M. (2025, August 26). Elon Musk's most ridiculous lie. *Gizmodo*. https://gizmodo.com/elon-musks-most-ridiculous-lie-2000647986

O'Connor, K. (2022). Constructivism, curriculum and the knowledge question: Tensions and challenges for higher education. *Studies in Higher Education*, *47*(2), 412–422.

O'Neil, C. (2017). *Weapons of math destruction: How big data increases inequality and threatens democracy*. Crown.

Ocumpaugh, J., Roscoe, R. D., Baker, R. S., Hutt, S., & Aguilar, S. J. (2024). Toward asset-based instruction and assessment in artificial intelligence in education. *International Journal of Artificial Intelligence in Education*, *34*(4), 1559–1598.

Olson, K. W. (1973). The GI Bill and higher education: Success and surprise. *American Quarterly*, *25*(5), 596–610.

Ohsaki, A., & Matsukawa, H. (2025). Interaction analysis between generative AI and high school students in scientific projects. In *Proceedings of the 18th international conference on Computer-Supported Collaborative Learning-CSCL 2025* (pp. 425–429). International Society of the Learning Sciences. Helsinki, Finland.

OpenAI. (2022, November). Introducing ChatGPT. *Openai.com*. https://openai.com/index/chatgpt/

Osterman, K. F. (2000). Students' need for belonging in the school community. *Review of Educational Research*, *70*(3), 323–367.

Pandolfo, N. (2012, January 24). As some schools plunge into technology, poor schools are left behind. *The Hechinger Report*. https://hechingerreport.org/as-some-schools-plunge-into-technology-poor-schools-are-left-behind/

Pani, B., Crawford, J., & Allen, K. A. (2024). Can generative artificial intelligence foster belongingness, social support, and reduce loneliness? A conceptual analysis. In Z. Lyu (Ed.), *Applications of generative AI* (pp. 261–276). Springer.

Paraschos, P. D., & Koulouriotis, D. E. (2023). Game difficulty adaptation and experience personalization: A literature review. *International Journal of Human–Computer Interaction*, *39*(1), 1–22.

Park, Y., & Jo, I. H. (2015). Development of the learning analytics dashboard to support students' learning performance. *Journal of Universal Computer Science*, *21*(1), 110.

Paul, A. (2024, May 24). Google's AI overview tells you to eat glue (Don't.). *Popular Science*. https://www.popsci.com/technology/google-ai-overview-wrong/

Peckham, J. (2025, May 7). Need more friends? Mark Zuckerberg says AI is the answer. *PCMAG*; PCMag. https://www.pcmag.com/news/need-more-friends-mark-zuckerberg-says-ai-is-the-answer

Pence, H. E., Hightower, G., Forlenza, J., Leonard, K., McLellan, A., Suero, A., ... & Pence, L. E. (2024). Using generative AI systems for critical thinking engagement in an advanced chemistry course: A case study. *Journal of Chemical Education*, *101*(9), 3789–3794.

Pickert, K. (2014, October 17). How the iPad helped bring down the Los Angeles schools chief. *Time*. https://time.com/3514155/ipad-john-deasy-lausd-superintendent-resigns/

Plato. (c. 399–347 BCE). Phaedrus. In J. M. Cooper (Ed.), *Complete works* (pp. 551–552). Hackett.

Polikoff, M. (2021). *Beyond standards: The fragmentation of education governance and the promise of curriculum reform* (Vol. 8). Cambridge, MA, USA: Harvard Education Press.

Polikoff, M., Michel-Herf, N., Avelar, J., Pillow, T., Pangelinan, C., & Casimere, H. (2024). State secrets: How transparent are state school report cards about the effects of COVID?. *Center on Reinventing Public Education*.

Polikoff, M., & Silver, D. (2022). Both supply and demand for COVID-related academic and social interventions are insufficient to address the negative effects of the pandemic: An essay for the learning curve. *Urban Institute*.

Portugal, I., Alencar, P., & Cowan, D. (2018). The use of machine learning algorithms in recommender systems: A systematic review. *Expert Systems with Applications*, *97*, 205–227.

Prasad, P., Balse, R., & Balchandani, D. (2025, April). Exploring multimodal generative AI for education through co-design workshops with students. In *Proceedings of the 2025 CHI* conference *on* human factors *in* computing systems (pp. 1–17). Yokohama, Japan.

Prilop, C. N., Mah, D. K., Jacobsen, L. J., Hansen, R. R., Weber, K. E., & Hoya, F. (2025). Generative AI in teacher education: Educators' perceptions of transformative potentials and the triadic nature of AI literacy explored through AI-enhanced methods. *Computers and Education: Artificial Intelligence*, *9*, 100471.

Pu, I., Ravi, P., Dinh, L. D., Joe, C., Ogoe, C., Li, Z., ... & Ostrowski, A. K. (2025). "How can we learn and use AI at the same time?": Participatory design of GenAI with high school students. In *Proceedings of the 24th* interaction design *and* children (pp. 204–220). Reykjavik, Iceland.

Pucillo, F., & Cascini, G. (2014). A framework for user experience, needs and affordances. *Design Studies*, *35*(2), 160–179.

Qadir, J., & Senturk, R. (2024). Educating for the AI era: Harnessing the wild genai horse through multiplex AI humanities and critical AI literacy. https://doi.org/10.2139/ssrn.5015109

Qian, K., Liu, S., Li, T., Raković, M., Li, X., Guan, R., ... & Gašević, D. (2025). Towards reliable generative AI-driven scaffolding: Reducing hallucinations and enhancing quality in self-regulated learning support. *Computers & Education*, *240*, 105448.

Radford, A., Wu, J., Child, R., Luan, D., Amodei, D., & Sutskever, I. (2019). Language models are unsupervised multitask learners. *OpenAI Blog*, *1*(8), 9.

Rafizadeh, N. (2025). Labor market adjustment to generative AI: The good, the bad, and the ugly. Available at *SSRN* 5367192.

Rathje, S., Ye, M., Globig, L. K., Pillai, R. M., Oldemburgo de Mello, V., & Van Bavel, J. J. (2025). Sycophantic AI increases attitude extremity and overconfidence [Pre-Print]. *OSF*. https://osf.io/5k6r9/

Ray, P. P. (2025). A review on vibe coding: Fundamentals, state-of-the-art, challenges and future directions. *Authorea Preprints*.

Reddit. (n.d.). *What is this thing?* [Online community]. Reddit. https://www.reddit.com/r/whatisthisthing/

Resnick, D., & Resnick, L. (1977). The nature of literacy: An historical exploration. *Harvard Educational Review*, *47*(3), 370–385.

Richmond, E. (2020, May 2). Shop class, over zoom. *The Atlantic*. https://www.theatlantic.com/education/archive/2020/05/remote-career-technical-school-covid-19-pandemic/611047/

Riley, N. S. (2018, February 11). Opinion | America's real digital divide. Nytimes.com; *The New York Times*. https://www.nytimes.com/2018/02/11/opinion/america-digital-divide.html?module=inline

Rizzo, A., Pasquini, A., Nucci, P. D., & Bagnara, S. (2000). SHELFS: Managing critical issues through experience feedback. *Human Factors and Ergonomics in Manufacturing & Service Industries*, *10*(1), 83–98.

Roberts, L. D., Howell, J. A., & Seaman, K. (2017). Give me a customizable dashboard: Personalized learning analytics dashboards in higher education. *Technology, Knowledge and Learning*, *22*(3), 317–333.

Rodway, P., & Schepman, A. (2023). The impact of adopting AI educational technologies on projected course satisfaction in university students. *Computers and Education: Artificial Intelligence*, *5*, 100150.

Rosario, A. (2025, September 3). I'm a high schooler. AI is demolishing my education. *The Atlantic*. https://www.theatlantic.com/technology/archive/2025/09/high-school-student-ai-education/684088/

Roser, M., & Ortiz-Ospina, E. (2018). Literacy. *Our world in data*. Retrieved from https://ourworldindata.org/literacy [Online Resource]

Ryan, R. M., & Deci, E. L. (2002). Overview of self-determination theory: An organismic dialectical perspective. In E. L. Deci & R. M. Ryan (Eds.), *Handbook of self-determination research* (pp. 3–33). University of Rochester Press.

Saini, M., Arora, V., Singh, M., Singh, J., & Adebayo, S. O. (2023). Artificial intelligence inspired multilanguage framework for note-taking and qualitative content-based analysis of lectures. *Education and Information Technologies*, *28*(1), 1141–1163.

Salari, N., Beiromvand, M., Hosseinian-Far, A., Habibi, J., Babajani, F., & Mohammadi, M. (2025). Impacts of generative artificial intelligence on the future of labor market: A systematic review. *Computers in Human Behavior Reports*, *18*, 100652.

Salhotra, P., & Rios, D. (2025, July 27). Alpha school, AI-Driven education founded in Austin, is coming to more cities. Nytimes.com; *The New York Times*. https://www.nytimes.com/2025/07/27/us/politics/ai-alpha-school-austin-texas.html

Santa Ana Unified School District. (2024, May). *SAUSD's artificial intelligence compass*. Santa Ana Unified School District.

Sapolsky, H. M., Crane, R. J., Neuman, W. R., & Noam, E. M. (Eds.). (2018). *The telecommunications revolution: Past, present and future*. Routledge.

Schuette, A. (2023). Navigating the enrollment cliff in higher education. Spotlight Report Brief. *Trellis Company*.

Schwartz, R. M., Schmitt, M. C., & Lose, M. K. (2012). Effects of teacher-student ratio in response to intervention approaches. *The Elementary School Journal, 112*(4), 547–567.

Sedrakyan, G., Malmberg, J., Verbert, K., Järvelä, S., & Kirschner, P. A. (2020). Linking learning behavior analytics and learning science concepts: Designing a learning analytics dashboard for feedback to support learning regulation. *Computers in Human Behavior, 107*, 105512.

Shabani, K., Khatib, M., & Ebadi, S. (2010). Vygotsky's zone of proximal development: Instructional implications and teachers' professional development. *English Language Teaching, 3*(4), 237–248.

Shen, X., Mo, X., & Xia, T. (2025). Exploring the attitude and use of GenAI-image among art and design college students based on TAM and SDT. *Interactive Learning Environments, 33*(2), 1198–1215.

Shin, N. (2003). Transactional presence as a critical predictor of success in distance learning. *Distance Education, 24*(1), 69–86. https://doi.org/10.1080/01587910303048

Shin, N., Choi, E., & Chang, S. (2024). Students' attitudes towards an AI-based interview for university admissions: Scale development and intervention effects. *Education and Information Technologies, 29*(15), 20055–20076.

Shu, K., Bhattacharjee, A., Alatawi, F., Nazer, T. H., Ding, K., Karami, M., & Liu, H. (2020). Combating disinformation in a social media age. *Wiley Interdisciplinary Reviews: Data Mining and Knowledge Discovery, 10*(6), e1385.

Sichel, D. E. (2001). *The computer revolution: An economic perspective.* Brookings Institution Press.

Sinatra, G. M., & Hofer, B. K. (2021). *Science denial: Why it happens and what to do about it.* Oxford University Press.

Slaten, C. D., Ferguson, J. K., Allen, K. A., Brodrick, D. V., & Waters, L. (2016). School belonging: A review of the history, current trends, and future directions. *The Educational and Developmental Psychologist, 33*(1), 1–15.

Smith, D. G. (2022, April). A 630-billion-word internet analysis shows "people" is interpreted as "men." *Scientific American.* https://www.scientificamerican.com/article/a-630-billion-word-internet-analysis-shows-people-is-interpreted-as-men/

Song, Y., Kim, J., Liu, Z., Li, C., & Xing, W. (2025). Students' perceived roles, opportunities, and challenges of a generative AI-powered teachable agent: a case of middle school math class. *Journal of Research on Technology in Education*, 1–19. https://doi.org/10.1080/15391523.2024.2447727

Sonnak, C., & Towell, T. (2001). The impostor phenomenon in British university students: Relationships between self-esteem, mental health, parental rearing style and socioeconomic status. *Personality and Individual Differences*, *31*(6), 863–874.

Stairs-Davenport, A. (2023). "Where do I start?" Inquiry into K-12 mainstream teachers' knowledge about differentiating instruction for ELLs in one US school district. *Education Inquiry*, *14*(2), 163–177.

Steele, C. M., & Aronson, J. (1995). Stereotype threat and the intellectual test performance of African Americans. *Journal of Personality and Social Psychology*, *69*(5), 797.

Steen, M. (2013). Co-design as a process of joint inquiry and imagination. *Design Issues*, *29*(2), 16–28.

Sticht, T. G. (2002). The rise of the adult education and literacy system in the United States: 1600–2000. *Office of Educational Research and Improvement*.

Subban, P., Suprayogi, M. N., Preston, M., Liyani, A. N., & Ratri, A. P. P. (2025). "Differentiation is sometimes a hit and miss". Educator perceptions of differentiated instruction in the higher education sector. *The Asia-Pacific Education Researcher*, *34*(3), 873–884.

Suthers, D., & Rosen, D. (2011, February). A unified framework for multi-level analysis of distributed learning. In *Proceedings of the 1st international conference on learning analytics and knowledge* (pp. 64–74). Banff, AB, Canada.

Tang, X., Chen, S., Cheng, Y., Chawla, N. V., Metoyer, R., & Ambrose, G. A. (2025). Understanding student attitudes and acceptability of GenAI tools in higher ed: Scale development and evaluation. *arXiv preprint* arXiv:2508.01926.

Teare, G. (2025, August 20). As funding to AI startups increases and concentrates, which investors have led? *Crunchbase News*. https://news.crunchbase.com/venture/big-dollar-ai-investors-2025-softbank/

Teplovs, C., Fujita, N., & Vatrapu, R. (2011, February). Generating predictive models of learner community dynamics. In *Proceedings of the 1st international conference on learning analytics and knowledge* (pp. 147–152). Banff, AB, Canada.

Tetzlaff, L., Schmiedek, F., & Brod, G. (2021). Developing personalized education: A dynamic framework. *Educational Psychology Review*, *33*(3), 863–882.

Thomson, J. J. (1976). Killing, letting die, and the trolley problem. *The Monist*, *59*(2), 204–217.

Tobisch, A., & Dresel, M. (2017). Negatively or positively biased? Dependencies of teachers' judgments and expectations based on students' ethnic and social backgrounds. *Social Psychology of Education*, *20*(4), 731–752.

Tomlinson, K., Jaffe, S., Wang, W., Counts, S., & Suri, S. (2025). Working with AI: Measuring the occupational implications of generative AI. *arXiv preprint* arXiv:2507.07935.

Tongchai, A., & Malakul, S. (2025). Thai teachers' perceptions of integrating generative AI in K-12 education: Opportunities and challenges. *TechTrends*, 1–13. https://doi.org/10.1007/s11528-025-01128-3

Vegas, E., & Winthrop, R. (2020, September 8). Beyond reopening schools: How education can emerge stronger than before COVID-19. *Brookings.* https://www.brookings.edu/articles/beyond-reopening-schools-how-education-can-emerge-stronger-than-before-covid-19/

Verbert, K., Duval, E., Klerkx, J., Govaerts, S., & Santos, J. L. (2013). Learning analytics dashboard applications. *American Behavioral Scientist*, *57*(10), 1500–1509.

Viberg, O., Hatakka, M., Bälter, O., & Mavroudi, A. (2018). The current landscape of learning analytics in higher education. *Computers in Human Behavior*, *89*, 98–110.

Villatoro Moral, S., & De Benito, B. (2021). An approach to co-design and self-regulated learning in technological environments. Systematic review. *Journal of New Approaches in Educational Research*, *10*(2), 234–250.

Vygotsky, L. S. (1978). *Mind in society: The development of higher psychological processes* (Vol. 86). Harvard University Press.

Wang, F., Li, N., Cheung, A. C., & Wong, G. K. (2025). In GenAI we trust: An investigation of university students' reliance on and resistance to generative AI in language learning. *International Journal of Educational Technology in Higher Education*, *22*(1), 59.

Warikoo, N., Sinclair, S., Fei, J., & Jacoby-Senghor, D. (2016). Examining racial bias in education: A new approach. *Educational Researcher*, *45*(9), 508–514.

Warschauer, M., Knobel, M., & Stone, L. (2004). Technology and equity in schooling: Deconstructing the digital divide. *Educational Policy*, *18*(4), 562–588.

Warschauer, M., & Matuchniak, T. (2010). New technology and digital worlds: Analyzing evidence of equity in access, use, and outcomes. *Review of Research in Education*, *34*(1), 179–225.

Watson, J. B. (2017). *Behaviorism*. Routledge.

Weber, M., & Baker, B. D. (2025). Does school funding matter in a pandemic? COVID-19 instructional models and school funding adequacy. *AERA Open*, *11*, 23328584251327581.

The White House. (2025a, April 23). Advancing artificial intelligence education for American youth. *The White House*. https://www.whitehouse.gov/presidential-actions/2025/04/advancing-artificial-intelligence-education-for-american-youth/

The White House. (2025b, January 23). Removing barriers to American leadership in artificial intelligence. *The White House*. https://www.whitehouse.gov/presidential-actions/2025/01/removing-barriers-to-american-leadership-in-artificial-intelligence/

Williamson, K., & Kizilcec, R. F. (2021, June). Learning analytics dashboard research has neglected diversity, equity and inclusion. In *Proceedings of the eighth ACM conference on learning@ scale* (pp. 287–290). New York, NY, USA.

Wilson, J. R. (2000). Fundamentals of ergonomics in theory and practice. *Applied Ergonomics*, *31*(6), 557–567.

Wittgenstein, L. (2009/1953). *Philosophical investigations*. John Wiley & Sons.

Witteveen, D., & Attewell, P. (2021). Delayed time-to-degree and post-college earnings. *Research in Higher Education*, *62*(2), 230–257.

Woo, S. E., LeBreton, J. M., Keith, M. G., & Tay, L. (2023). Bias, fairness, and validity in graduate-school admissions: A psychometric perspective. *Perspectives on Psychological Science*, *18*(1), 3–31.

Xing, Y., & Aguilar, S. J. (2026). Early insights on promoting critical thinking with an AI coach for argumentative writing. In *Proceedings of the 2025* connected learning summit. Online.

Xiu, R. L., & Aguilar, S. J. (2026). Instructor-led generative artificial intelligence (GenAI) interventions vs. unstructured student-initiated use in post-secondary education: A systematic literature review. In *Proceedings of the 2025 connected learning summit*. Online.

Yang, A., & Cui, J. (2025, August 7). OpenAI releases GPT-5, calling it a "team of Ph.D. level experts in your pocket." *NBC News*. https://www.nbcnews.com/tech/tech-news/openai-releases-chatgpt-5-rcna223265

Yilmaz, R., & Yilmaz, F. G. K. (2023). The effect of generative artificial intelligence (AI)-based tool use on students' computational thinking skills, programming self-efficacy and motivation. *Computers and Education: Artificial Intelligence*, *4*, 100147.

Young, M. F., Slota, S., Cutter, A. B., Jalette, G., Mullin, G., Lai, B., ... & Yukhymenko, M. (2012). Our princess is in another castle: A review of trends in serious gaming for education. *Review of Educational Research, 82*(1), 61–89.

Yusuf, A., Pervin, N., & Román-González, M. (2024). Generative AI and the future of higher education: A threat to academic integrity or reformation? Evidence from multicultural perspectives. *International Journal of Educational Technology in Higher Education, 21*(1), 21.

Zhang, L., Liu, X., & Hu, Y. (2024). Degrees of return: Estimating internal rates of return for college majors using quantile regression. *American Educational Research Journal, 61*(3), 577–609.

Zheng, C., Yuan, K., Guo, B., Hadi Mogavi, R., Peng, Z., Ma, S., & Ma, X. (2024, May). Charting the future of AI in project-based learning: A Co-design exploration with students. In *Proceedings of the 2024 CHI conference on human factors in computing systems* (pp. 1–19). Honolulu, HI, USA.

Zhou, E. P. (2023, October). The fallibility of AI content detectors. In *2023 IEEE MIT undergraduate research technology conference* (URTC) (pp. 1–4).

Zhou, R., Huang, H., Zhang, G., Zhou, H., & Bian, J. (2025). Crash-based safety testing of autonomous vehicles: Insights from generating safety-critical scenarios based on in-depth crash data. *IEEE Transactions on Intelligent Transportation Systems, 26*(10), 15616–15630.

Index

About the Author

Dr. Stephen J. Aguilar is Associate Professor of Education at the USC Rossier School of Education and leads USC's Center for Generative AI and Society. His research focuses on investigating how emerging and established educational technologies influence teaching, learning, and motivation. Currently, he is focused on better understanding the effects of Generative AI tools on students and educators worldwide.

His honors and awards include winning the Wilbert J. McKeachie Early Career Award for Motivation in Education Research and the American Educational Research Association (AERA) Division C Early Career Award. His work has been funded by the National Science Foundation, the American Educational Research Association (AERA), the National Institutes of Health, and the US Army Research Office, among others.

Dr. Aguilar has also given televised interviews of his work in both English and Spanish, has been a guest on NPR's *AirTalk*, and has been interviewed by the *Los Angeles Times*, the *New York Times*, *USA Today*, *The Atlantic*, *Bloomberg*, and the *Washington Post*. His work during the pandemic also informed California Assembly Bill No. 1176, which provided much-needed subsidies for families in need of broadband internet. The resulting Affordable Connectivity Program has helped over one million families afford reliable high-speed internet during the pandemic and beyond.

Dr. Aguilar received a BA in Philosophy and Psychology from Georgetown University, an MA in the Humanities (Philosophy) from the University of Chicago, and a PhD in Education and Psychology from the University of Michigan. Previously, he taught sixth and seventh grade in East Palo Alto, California, and served as Director of Institute Technology for Teach For America–Los Angeles's summer institute.

www.ingramcontent.com/pod-product-compliance
Ingram Content Group UK Ltd.
Pitfield, Milton Keynes, MK11 3LW, UK
UKHW021417090826
474190UK00001B/24

9 798216 438564